First published in the United States of America in 2002
by UNIVERSE PUBLISHING
A Division of Rizzoli International Publications, Inc.
300 Park Avenue South
New York, NY 10010

2002 2003 2004 2005 2006 / 10 9 8 7 6 5 4 3 2 1

Printed and bound in France by Pollina - n° L86999

ISBN 0-7893-0817-7

Library of Congress Catalog Control Number: 2002107729

Original title:	Cuisines des Pays de France: Histoires et Recettes
Text by:	Jean-Luis André
Recipes by:	Jean-François Mallet
Photographs by:	Jean–Daniel Sudres
Published by:	Les Editions du Chêne — Hachette Livre 2001

French Edition
Editor:	Nathalie Bailleux
Artistic Direction:	Sabine Houplain
Design:	Chine
Proofreading:	Isabelle Macé

U.S. Edition
Editor:	Elizabeth Smith
Jacket Designer:	Amelia Costigan
Typesetting:	Cindy Poorbaugh
Proofreading:	Ilaria Fusina

Translated from the French by Elizabeth Heard

This book was published with the help of the French Ministry of Culture-National Book Office

Dishes of France

Text by
JEAN-LOUIS ANDRÉ

Recipes and
culinary direction by
JEAN-FRANÇOIS MALLET

Photographs by
JEAN-DANIEL SUDRES

*an insider's tour
of the regions and
recipes*

UNIVERSE

Contents

Landscapes and their Flavors   6

the northwest   10
Lobster *à l'armoricaine*   12
Sole normande in Dieppe   18
The *crêpes* and *galettes* of Brittany   26
Tarte aux pommes in Normandy   36
Traditional recipes of the Northwest   44

the northeast   46
Moules-frites in the North   48
Onion soup in Paris   56
Choucroute in Alsace   62
Traditional recipes of the Northeast   70

the center   72
Bœuf bourguignon in the Charolais   74
Estofinado in Aveyron   82
Aligot and *truffade* in the Auvergne   90
Potée in the Auvergne   98
Traditional recipes of the Center   106

the southeast   108
Bouillabaisse in Marseille   110
Fondue in Savoie   118
Poulet à la crème in Bresse   126
Pissaladière in Nice   134
Fiadone in Corsica   142
Traditional recipes of the Southeast   150

the southwest   152
Cassoulet in Castelnaudary   154
Confit in Gers   162
Poule au pot in Béarn   170
Basquaise in the Basque country   178
Traditional recipes of the Southwest   186

Resources   188
Index of recipes with English translations 191

Landscapes and their Flavors

Here are twenty traditional French dishes, each with its own story. As you savor them, you will encounter a myriad of personalities, kitchen secrets, tricks of the trade, rituals, and recipes in their infinite variations. We have not tried to track down the most esoteric specialties, or mere local curiosities...quite the contrary. For our point of departure we used those emblematic local dishes that are like souvenir postcards, mailed so often that we lose track of their origins and forget what they can tell us about ourselves. We have visited artisans of the kitchen in country inns where each day's *plat du jour* is redolent of the countryside itself. We have quizzed mothers and grandmothers on the secrets of their kitchens. We have shared the enthusiasm of a grower who compares his potatoes to truffles, and a diary farmer who ranks his cream and butter as the equals of caviar. We have given human faces to our classic dishes.

Twenty dishes to represent a nation—from one perspective, a good many, from another, very few. Very few when you dwell upon the subtle variations across each region, as do many culinary cultists in relentless quest of absolute orthodoxy. But the underlying themes linking these dishes together are readily apparent. Consider *poule au pot*, for example. Its origins clearly lie in Béarn, but the notion of cooking meats and vegetables together in a pot over a low fire is as old as mankind. Henri IV's favorite dish is really a first cousin of the Auvergneſs *potée*, which in turn is not so distantly related to Marseille's *bouillabaisse*. *Pissaladière* is certainly not confined to Nice: just change a few ingredients and the flat bread, toasted golden in a wood burning oven, becomes *pizza* or *fougasse*, just a few steps removed. Brittany's legendary *crêpes* are known elsewhere as *brick*, *aumonières*, or *pancakes* and they sizzle on griddles all over France to mark the religious feast of Chandeleur, Christ's presentation in the Temple. Is all this really so surprising? The motivating factor is the same everywhere—to transform the mundane and often meager into a dish worthy of a king.

In the words of Georges Simenon, « Most recipes are basically born of necessity. If there had been refrigerators in the Middle Ages... »

Facing page
Bouillabaisse is served on the terrace of the Grand Bar des Goudes in Marseille.

Left
Cabbage, an indispensable ingredient in Auvergnat *potée*.

Purists who cling to regional traditionalism may shudder, but we should face the facts. French cuisine is a long story of interchanges, crossbreeding, and hybridization. Consider ingredients that seem to have been with us forever. Buckwheat, that essential component of the *crêpes* of Quimper, came straight back from the East with the Crusaders. The dried cod used to make the *estofinado* in Decazeville harks back to the story of Norwegian cod fishermen by way of the River Lot and the Atlantic Ocean. Lobster dishes of Lorient, like the *bouillabaisse* of Marseille, include the spices that sailors bartered with when they returned from distant voyages. Basque *piperade* calls for hot red peppers, brought to France from the Americas by the Spanish conquistadors. The same goes for the tomato, now the queen of Mediterranean cuisine, and corn, without which *foie gras* and *confit* would be very different from what they are...and even beans. Consider beans: they are prepared all over southwestern France following a recipe of Arab origin, which is not to detract a whit from the hearty local accent of our good old *cassoulet*.

There is another artificial boundary that separates rustic cooking from the more polished, even aristocratic, approach whose rules were set forth in Escoffier's heyday. The truth is that the cuisines are mutually dependent. The celebrated *sole normande*, for example, is a cooking school invention, probably introduced by a few Parisian restaurants in the nineteenth century. Nevertheless, the dish incorporates genuinely local ingredients, and so when the vogue for it passed in the capital, it could still be had in Normandy's seaside restaurants. Fishermen's *bouillabaisse* doubtless began as a simple *court bouillon*, but after a detour through the Belle Époque's most opulent households, the bouillon became a rich man's soup embellished with rockfish. These developments certainly did not diminish the popularity of *bouillabaisse* with the common folk. *Fondue* no doubt gained a great deal in the course of its migration from alpine chalets to Brillat-Savarin's sumptuous table.

You will discover all these traditional recipes in the pages that follow. Because cuisine is constantly in transition, by its very nature alive and always evolving, we have also invited some of the greatest chefs to improvise and create dishes based on the well-loved, widely shared foundation of these recipes. Collaborating with Jean-Daniel Sudres and Jean-François Mallet, we have charted our own paths and devised our own recipes. And so the journey through time and space comes full circle.

Facing page
The Brionnais countryside, home of Charolais beef.

Above
Cheese molds in the Auvergne.

Left
Truffade tart.

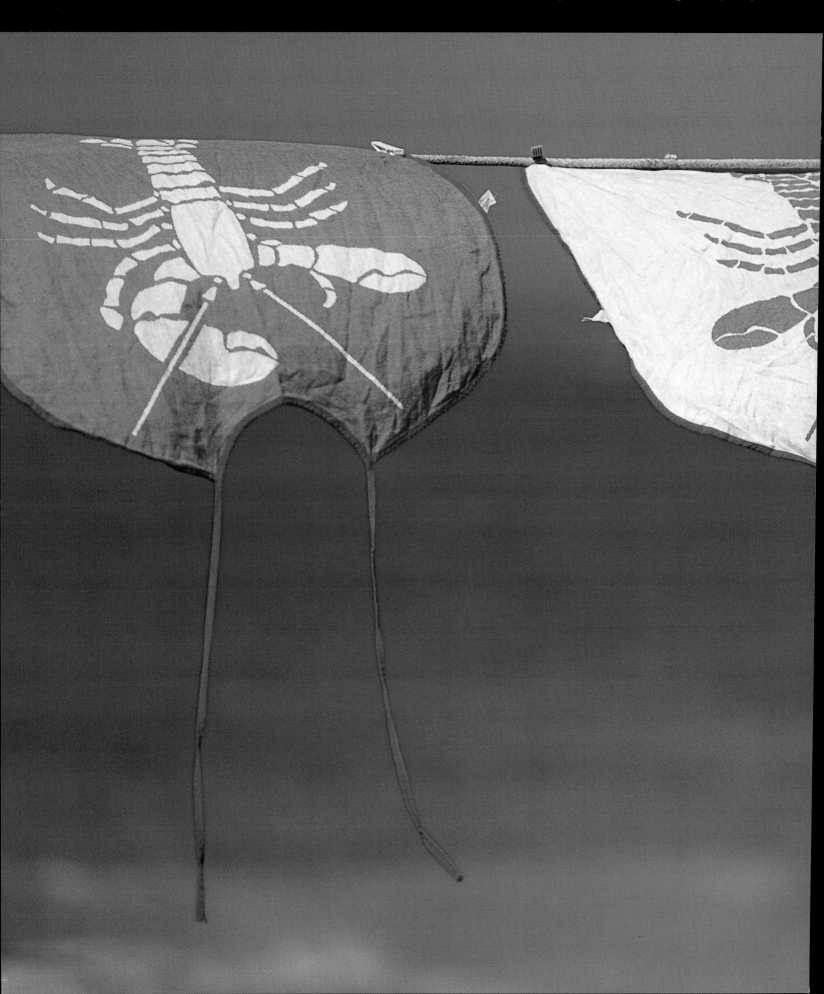

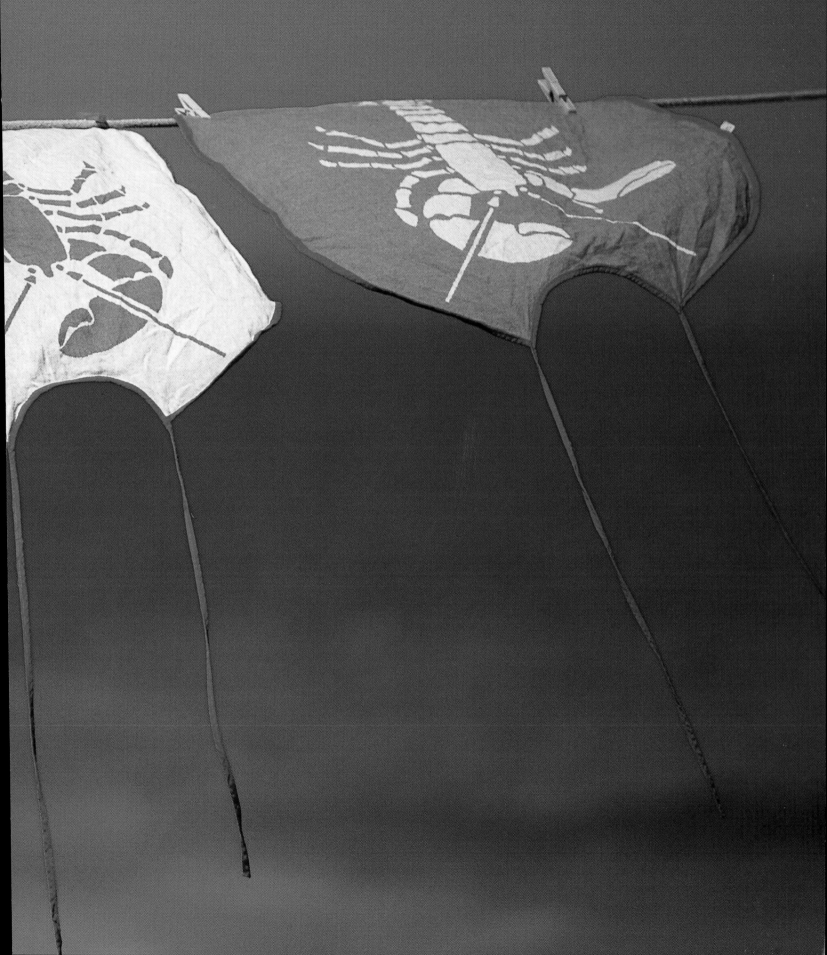

Lobster
à l'armoricaine

Armoricaine or *américaine*? It's an open question, but look beyond the debates over the name, and the truth is inescapable: the most flavorful lobsters have always come from Brittany. For centuries they have been prepared throughout the peninsula boiled up in cauldrons or stewed in *ragoûts*, sometimes blending the briny taste of the sea with the fragrance of spices from the East.

Above
Breton lobsters are blue in deep sea waters, but they turn a brilliant red when cooked, earning them the name « Cardinals of the Sea.»

Facing page
A fisherman's house at land's end on the northern coast of Brittany.

The Breton lobster's exalted reputation has never been disputed. Its fame extended to the English and French courts, and the *Gazetin du comestible* urged its Parisian readers to order this « crayfish of the sea ready to serve » in 1767. Soon Paris could not survive without the « cardinals of the sea », so christened by the nineteenth-century chronicler Monselet in homage to the brilliant red that the crustacean's shell turns when it is cooked. You can still see the old lobster tanks built in the 1930s near Lorient by that very Parisian restaurant Prunier. In those days the tanks, surrounded by low walls at sea level with tunnels and locks carved from the rock, were a highly efficient production center designed to satisfy year-round demand from gourmets who were as numerous as they were demanding.

Although many of these sought-after crustaceans were exported with due ceremony, some gastronomes preferred to relish them on their home turf. The restaurant Chez Melanie in Riec-sur-Belon, not far from Pont-Aven, had its heyday in the Roaring Twenties, finally closing in the mid-1970s for lack of an heir. Its specialty? The lobster prepared by Melanie, a simple farmer's wife, later the village grocer, who subsequently assumed the stature of a goddess of Breton cooking. She cooked the dish without ever doffing her traditional lace coiffe. Melanie's close friend, Curnonsky, the « prince of gastronomes », Colette, and later Georges Pompidou, all made countless trips to Riec to relish this lobster *ragoût*.

> « Lobster is the essence of the Brittany that Parisians love: briny, invigorating, and embodying all the delights of the sea. »

In the 1960s and 1970s, speedy refrigerated transport facilitated the importation of Canadian and other North American lobsters, but Brittany's reputation was merely enhanced by the competition. Today as yesterday, no other lobster comes close to matching the flavor of those harvested along the Côtes-d'Armor or the Cornouaille coast.

À *l'armoricaine* or à *l'américaine*?
Like the crustacean itself, the story of the origins of the most frequently prepared lobster recipe shifts between Brittany and Paris. Legend has it that the recipe is actually « *à l'américaine* », invented one evening in 1858 at Peter's a Parisian restaurant in the Passage des Princes.

Lobster *à l'armoricaine*

Serves 6
Preparation time : 45 minutes
Cooking time : 1 hour 10 minutes

6 live Breton lobsters, weighing 2 lbs.
each
5 shallots
2 sprigs of tarragon
3 tomatoes
1 *bouquet garni*
3 1/2 oz. lightly salted butter
8 1/2 oz. liquid *crème fraîche*
4 tablespoons tomato paste
3 1/2 oz. olive oil
8 1/2 oz. white wine
8 1/2 oz. fish stock (You may also use
freeze dried fish stock.)
1 tablespoon flour
3 tablespoons Cognac
salt and pepper

1- Plunge the lobsters into boiling water for 5 minutes to kill them. Separate the heads from the bodies. Remove the soft « coral » from the heads with a small spoon and combine it with the butter.

2- Peel and slice the shallots, rinse the tarragon, and cut the tomatoes into large dice. Heat the olive oil in a large pot and cook the lobster heads over high heat. Flambé the head with Cognac, then add the shallots, tomatoes, *bouquet garni*, and tarragon.

3- Add salt and pepper to taste. Crush the heads in the pot with a mortar. Lower the heat and cook, stirring, over low heat for 5 minutes. Add the flour and tomato paste, combine with the seasonings and pour the white wine over all.

4- Reduce the wine by half, add the fish stock and let it simmer over low heat for 30 minutes. Add the *crème fraîche*. Cook, stirring, for another 10 minutes. Put the sauce through a fine strainer. Pour it into another pot and re-heat. Add the tails and claws to the hot sauce and let them cook 10 minutes.

5- Remove the claws and tails and drain them. Crack the claws with a hammer. Cut the tails in half lengthwise. Arrange the tails and claws on a serving platter.

6- Add the coral-flavored butter to the warm sauce and stir gently until it melts. Correct the seasoning. Cover the lobster pieces with the sauce and serve immediately.

Les petits homards de Olivier Rœllinger

Olivier Rœllinger, the chef of the Michelin two star restaurant « Les Maisons de Bricourt » in Cancale, prepares lobster in a spiced sauce. « It is essential to cook the lobster gently and very briefly so that it maintains its consistency and keeps all its flavor. » The spices required can be purchased from specialty food shops.

1- Sweat the ginger and galangal, finely diced, with the allspice, vanilla bean, mace, and nutmeg. After 2 minutes, add the mushrooms, washed and chopped. Pour in 1 3/4 oz. of water and add the tamarind paste, the *annatto* oil, the lime leaves, the garlic, and salt and pepper to taste. Simmer for 30 minutes, then strain the broth through a sieve and set aside.

2- Poach the live lobsters in the spiced bouillon for 10 minutes and remove from heat. Drain the lobsters and cut them in half lengthwise. Remove the coral from the heads with a small spoon and add it to the bouillon. Let the coriander infuse in the warm bouillon. Separate the lobster claws from the bodies. Keep the half lobsters and claws warm.

3- Cut the mango into very small pieces.

4- Reheat the bouillon over low heat, add the lime juice, and whisk in the butter. Arrange the lobster halves, claws, and pieces of mango on a large platter, strain the sauce, and cover the lobster meat and mangos with it.

Serve very hot over rice.

Serves 6
Preparation time : 40 minutes
Cooking time : 45 minutes

3 live Breton lobsters, weighing 2 lbs. each
1 3/4 oz. fresh ginger
1 ounce fresh galangal (in ginger family)
1/4 of a nutmeg, grated
1 pinch of mace
1/4 ounce allspice
1 teaspoon red *annatto* oil
1/2 vanilla bean
10 small white mushrooms
juice of 1 lime
1/2 mango
5 lime leaves
3 1/2 oz. olive oil
3/4 ounce tamarind paste
3 sprigs of fresh coriander
1 clove of garlic, blanched
1 3/4 oz. butter
salt and pepper

La salade de fruits de mer, vinaigrette à l'armoricaine

Recipes *à l'américaine* and *à l'armoricaine* both refer to shellfish preparations in a sauce based on tomatoes, garlic, shellfish juices, and oil.

1- Peel and slice the shallots and crush the garlic cloves, leaving the skin on. Wash and dice the tomatoes and celery. Cut the heads off the shrimp, and carefully remove the meat from the tails. Refrigerate the shrimp and the scallops.

2- Heat 3 tablespoons of the oil in a deep frying pan. Cook the heads and shells in the oil briefly over high heat, then let them color over slow heat, stirring. Add the thyme, shallots, and garlic cloves. Crush the heads with a rolling pin, then put them back in the sauté pan. Cook them 10 minutes over low heat. Remove the pan from the heat, add the rest of the oil to the pan, cover with food wrap, and allow the shells to infuse in the warm oil for 1 hour.

3- Strain the flavored oil, pressing down hard to get the shellfish juices as well as the celery, garlic, and shallot flavors. Warm 2 tablespoons of seasoned oil in a frying pan. Cook the scallops and shrimp over high heat 1 minute on each side. Add the diced tomato and celery, cook 2 minutes longer, and add salt and pepper to taste.

4- Cut the lettuce hearts in half and put them on individual plates. Arrange the scallops, shrimp, tomatoes, and the warm, crunchy celery on top.

5- Emulsify the warm shrimp oil with the green mustard and vinegar in a food processor. Pour this vinaigrette over the salads and serve.

Serves 6
Preparation : 20 minutes
Resting time : 1 hour
Cooking time : 15 minutes

18 large shrimp
12 large scallops
2 shallots
2 garlic cloves
6 hearts of lettuce
4 tomatoes
1 celery stalk
1 sprig of thyme
5 oz. sunflower oil
1 teaspoon green mustard
1 teaspoon cider vinegar
salt and pepper

One evening, Pierre Fraisse, the owner of Peter's was visited by a group of Americans near closing time. There was nothing left in the pantry but live lobsters, and the chef had to improvise. He cut the lobsters up, plunged them into hot oil with tomatoes, garlic, white wine, shallots, and pepper and sent them into the dining room. The guests were delighted, and asked the name of the dish; the owner didn't hesitate: « These lobsters are your very own. They are *à l'américaine*. » The tale may be too good to be true, but plenty of ink has flowed recounting it over time. Another Parisian restaurateur later claimed he had invented the dish fifteen years before the idea ever occurred to Fraisse.

Others have supported the contrarian view that the preparation has Breton origins. Around 1900, Prosper Montagné, the creator of the *Larousse Gastronomique*, omitted the term « *à l'américaine* », and swore by lobster « *à l'armoricaine* », while the paper *Gil Blas* claimed to have unearthed the original recipe in the notebooks of a chef from Saint-Paul-de-Léon just before World War I.

In Brittany, the locals just smile. « I know that these days people prepare lobsters in a more contemporary way, simply grilled, but in my opinion there's no substitute for

« I eat lobsters for holiday feasts, birthdays, to celebrate any important occasion. »

a good *armoricaine*, » says Alain le Bras, a fisherman. The man knows whereof he speaks. Like his father before him, he goes to drop his lobster traps between the rocks and islands of Finistère-Nord in the first fair days of June when the water begins to warm up. Eighty lobster traps (once made of wicker, but plastic these days), are tied up and filled with a generous amount of bait. The *Renard des mers*, a tiny boat, heads toward the Pierres Noires lighthouse in the heart of the Regional Park of Armorica. The catch is good and the lobster traps are full. There are a few spider crabs, some larger crabs, and about twenty lobsters, which the fisherman pulls out cautiously. He wraps a rubber band around the claws and applies a seal to the shell to confirm their authenticity.

It is important to make a clear distinction between native lobsters and those imported from North America, Ireland, and Scotland. The authentic ones

are sold through an organization created six years ago, the Association of French Coast Lobstermen. Reserved for the truly privileged, these lobsters are naturally more expensive, and Brittany produces less than 220 tons a year of them.

Dreams of the exotic East

Next stop, Paris. Paradoxically, the cooking trend here shies away from the good old *á l'armoricaine* preparation that the capital was once so eager to claim as its own. Now it is considered a disgrace to cover something naturally so delicately flavored with sauce and seasonings…to overcook it…not to separate the meat from the coral, which can be put to such good use in other recipes. Patrons at the finest tables prefer that chefs roast a lobster and serve it unadorned, or even *tartare*, accompanied by a *velouté* of cabbage and *crème aux cèpes*, as does the star-spangled chef Jean-Marie Guilbaud, who presides over the restaurant Ferme du Letty in Bénodet.

These faddish cravings have their day, and the heated polemics fade into the distance as we return to Brittany, where people continue to consume lobster *ragoûts*, *à l'armoricaine*, or otherwise, as they always

have. Not far from the Pointe du Raz, on the road to the Pointe du Van, the people of Cléden-Cap-Sizun have been treating themselves to stewed lobster in coral cream sauce at the restaurant l'Étrave for over thirty years. Huguette Roma still follows the recipe passed down by her mother. « On the île de Sein, where many *caseyeurs* used to live, lobster was always prepared in a *ragoût* like this. It's the lobster's coral and that oil between the flesh and the shell that gives the sauce its salmon color. » This delicacy is served here with the same generous hand as a *civet de lapin* would be elsewhere.

Near Lorient, lobster is prepared with curry. Here is something Parisians and Bretons might agree upon: *l'armoricaine* could be a Creole dish in its origin, Hispano-Cuban-Floridian-Louisianan. It is possible when we consider the presence of tomato, an immigrant from South America, spices, and spirits (*eau-de-vie* or *Cognac*) used to flambé the golden sautéed lobster pieces. This is the essence of Brittany, a land open to the four winds. There was a time when Lorient was still called l'Orient. No doubt the ship owners and notables of the long-gone Compagnie des Indes regaled themselves with lobster banquets.

Sole normande in Dieppe

Sole is Norman, but *sole normande* is Parisian. The dish was devised in the capital by good home cooks in Balzac's era, and the recipe remains the ultimate classic in every hotel school. Now Normans are finally rediscovering for themselves the distinctive flavors of their own region.

Above
In Yport in the Seine-Maritime region, men still use old fashioned techniques to fish for sole near the shore. They embark in small boats called « canots » or « dories », which they drag onto the beach at the end of the day, since there is no real harbor here.

Below
This shoreline, called the « estran » by people in Caux, is rimmed by chalk cliffs. This environment is ideal for sole, which flourish in these shallow, mildly saline waters.

« We simply want you to eat, and my husband too; pass the sole back to the gentleman, you can see his is cold… » Thus sole makes its appearance in *Swann's Way*. Did Proust himself sample it under the chandeliers of the Grand Hotel in Cabourg, or at a dinner party in the Faubourg-Saint-Germain? We will never know. Whatever the answer, restaurants along the coast of Normandy have inscribed this outdated trophy of home cooking at the top of their menus. *Sole normande* no longer calls to mind family reunions; now it evokes the flavors of a weekend by the sea and the briny air at the end of the Autoroute de l'Ouest.

A beauty with middle class pretensions in the Pays de Caux

Is sole really a local treasure? People here, between Mont-Saint-Michel and the Baie de Somme, just smile when you ask. Perhaps it is, but it has been so for far less time than you might suppose.

The port of Dieppe, for example, has long been celebrated for its herring production and its distant expeditions to catch cod, and more recently, for its miraculous harvest of scallops. People have fished here for abundant sole and many other species; since the Middle Ages. This flatfish prefers sandy bottoms in shallow, mildly saline water: conditions at the foot of the white cliffs of the Pays de Caux are ideal. There has always been an array of ingenious ways to catch them, using tridents, traps, nets, and long lines strung with well over a hundred hooks. But no one ever really attached a

matic origin. Normans are now happy to boast of the virtues of their « very own local » sole, which of course is completely unrelated to the fish caught by Dutch fishermen a few nautical miles away.

> « The flavor of sauce à la crème *evokes the softly rolling inland countryside, with its grazing cattle and pastures crisscrossed with hedges.* »

The fishmonger lays out about a hundred kilograms of fish on her stall, in front of the big boat basin on the quay. Like her ancestors, she sells her husband's catch. The fishing boats lined up behind her bear names that are wordplays on the sea itself: the *Battant*, the *Calypso*, the *Princesse des mers*. The bars on the quay have names like Le Retour or Le Coup de Roulis, and their painted signs are faded by the fog that rolls in from the sea. Dieppe is a real fishing port with a daily auction of the day's catch. Its men head out to sea, sometimes for a couple of days and sometimes for many weeks. Dieppe retains its feeling of the open sea, and its fishermen still cast off at dawn to trawl, net, and stow their catch in the holds of their boats. Some of the credit goes to Paris. If *sole normande*, or even *sole dieppoise*, now make for good times in Normandy, that is thanks to the capital as well.

great deal of importance to sole. It was not to be found on the list of « royal fish » that were forbidden to fishermen and reserved for monastic consumption. At the end of the seventeenth century, the weighty *Encyclopédie des pêches* by Duhamel du Monceau, which makes much of delicacies concocted from turbot and *barbue*, mentions sole only in passing.

Times have indeed changed since then. The Hôtel des Arcades, one of Dieppe's grandest hostelries, offers its *sole dieppoise* every day, a tradition of enig-

La sole normande

This is the classic recipe for the *sole normande* that Christian Constant served in the Hôtel Crillon in Paris. When this dish was at its peak popularity in the great Parisian restaurants, chefs added sliced truffles warmed in Madeira to the plate at the last moment.

Serves 6
Preparation time : 1 hour 30 minutes
Cooking time : 45 minutes

6 small soles (prepared by your fishmonger)
6 medium-sized smelt or gudgeons
1 quart cultivated mussels
7 oz. shelled red shrimp
6 oysters
6 crayfish
7 oz. white wine
5 oz. butter
2 oz. *crème fraîche*
1 cup milk
1 egg plus 1 egg yolk
6 white mushrooms
2 shallots
1 *bouquet garni*
11/2 tbsp. flour
11/2 tbsp. soft breadcrumbs
salt and pepper
deep fryer

1- Pre-heat the oven to 350°. Put the mussels, white wine, and *bouquet garni* in a large pot and cook 5 minutes to open the mussels. Turn off the heat, drain the mussels, and remove them from their shells. Strain and set aside the cooking juices.

2- Clean the mushrooms and cook them whole in 1 ounce of butter and 2 tablespoons of water. Mix their cooking juices with the mussel juices and keep the mushrooms warm. Open the oysters, drain them, and chop them up. Peel and slice the shallots.

3- Place the sole on an ovenproof platter with the chopped shallots. Cover them with the cooking juices, chopped oysters, and the rest of the butter, cut up into small pieces. Salt and pepper to taste and bake in the oven for 25 minutes.

4- Immerse the shrimp in boiling water for 4 minutes. Remove the meat from the tails, leaving the heads on.

5- Beat the whole egg as you would for an omelet. Dip the gudgeons or smelts in the beaten egg, then in milk, flour, and finally breadcrumbs.
Fry them and keep them warm.

6- Remove the sole from the oven, drain, and place on a serving plate. Arrange the crayfish, fried fish, and mushroom caps on top.
Reduce the cooking juices with the *crème fraîche*, the shrimp, and the mussels. Remove from heat and whisk the egg yolk into the warm sauce to thicken it.

7- Correct the seasoning of the sauce. Cover the sole, smelt, crayfish, and mushroom caps with the very hot *sauce normande*. Serve immediately with rice.
You may also serve the mussels in their shells for a more formal presentation.

Fishmongers in Dieppe naturally give sole a privileged place.

deep sea to their hearts' content, now that all of France was waiting to receive their harvest.

This was also the era when Normandy became fashionable and casinos thrived next to swimming establishments. The English, French, and Russian aristocracy held court at the seaside and splashed along the shore at low tide. Here *sole normande* was born. By 1840, it was a specialty (admittedly one of two hundred specialties) at the Rocher de Cancale, a prominent restaurant where Balzac liked to place the various characters of his *Comédie Humaine*. Langlais, its chef, codified the recipe, no doubt adapting a wine sauce served several years earlier in Carême's restaurant.

> « *Every day the* trains de marée *depart from Dieppe's new railroad station, and every mouth in les Halles starts watering.* »

Despite its provincial origins, the dish attained an honored place in culinary circles which it maintains to this day. Christian Constant, former chef at the Crillon, made it an obligatory menu offering until he retired. *Les Bases de la cuisine* by Planche and Sylvestre, which is the bible of aspiring chefs, has a picture of *sole normande* on its jacket. As *sole dieppoise*, a more refined adaptation, the dish became the final examination in hotel schools. Cutting the filets, trimming the mushrooms, cooking the shellfish, reducing the bouillon while preserving the delicate texture of the fish–these are the techniques that must be mastered as the basis for truly great French cuisine.

Giving credit where credit is due— to Paris

The Norman coast has always made its living from expeditions to distant locales. Since the twelfth century, the legendary *chasse-marées* set off from here on missions to provide supplies to Paris.

The men drove horses and mules ahead of them, whence the name *chasse-marée*. Later the Normans set out in huge carts pulled by teams of four or six powerful workhorses, stopping five or six times at staging points along the way to get fresh horses. They covered some forty leagues in about thirty hours, and the fish were delivered fresh because people already knew how to preserve them with ice. Parisian nomenclature commemorates this trade; where these journeys ended, there is both a « rue de Poissonniers » and a « faubourg Poissonnière.» The railroad came in 1848. The fishermen of Dieppe could work the English Channel, trawling the

The finest flower of the Norman countryside

Calling this national dish *normande*, or even *dieppoise*, is accurate. Consider the use of cream, without which Norman cuisine would not exist. « It has always been a part of fishermen's diets, » explains Eric Tavernier, the author of *150 Years of Fishing in Dieppe* and chairman of the Cité de la Mer in Dieppe. Farmers from inland Normandy brought cream to coastal residents on market days; the large Saturday market is a legacy of this tradition. It was often bartered for herring. Cream was relatively inexpensive, certainly compared to butter. In fact, sailors called the boat owners and captains «butter gluttons.»

Cream is an ingredient in *sole normande* of course,

along with shrimp and mussels, small shellfish that women until very recently gathered at low tide.

Even the mushrooms known as *champignons de Paris* had long been a local specialty. The cliffs near Dieppe are riddled with curious excavations. The old people still recall the wretched souls, impoverished fishermen, and stone gatherers who were displaced when the channel was cut through and lived there until World War II. « When those people arrived in the shelters, » continues Eric Tavernier, «that ended the cultivation of mushrooms there. »

Products of one region are deployed in the recipes of another. Eventually Dieppe embraced the dish baptized in its honor. Ever since, the chamber of commerce has organized an annual *sole dieppoise* contest in which students from all over Europe compete.

Above
Sailors' bars in Dieppe used to be called Le Retour or Le Coup de roulis. These days they flaunt the name of the local specialty.

Left
Sole may be brown or yellow, but they are generally cooked without their skins, which a fishmonger removes with a sure hand.

Les filets de sole à la dieppoise

1- Combine the mussels, the shallots and half the white wine in a pot. Cook over high heat for 5 minutes, stirring constantly, to open the mussels. Drain the mussels, remove the meat from the shells, and put them aside on a platter. Strain and reserve the cooking juices.

2- Wash and quarter the mushrooms. Sauté them in 1 ounce butter and set aside with the shelled mussels.

3- Combine the remaining white wine with the fish stock in a large pot and bring to a boil. Immerse the filets in the simmering liquid for 3 minutes, then drain and place them on a large earthenware platter. Arrange the shrimp, mussels, and mushrooms on the platter.

4- Add the mussels' cooking juices to the sole cooking juices and reduce them to 3/4 of their original volume. Add the *crème fraîche* and reduce by half over low heat. Add salt and pepper to taste.

5- 20 minutes before serving, add small pieces of the chilled butter to the warm sauce, whisking to blend. Cover the sole filets, mussels, shrimp, and mushrooms with the sauce, and brown 5 minutes under the broiler.

6- Serve the filets de s*ole à la dieppoise* very hot, accompanied by white rice.

Serves 8
Preparation time : 40 minutes
Cooking time : 45 minutes

16 sole filets
1/4 cup white wine
1/4 cup fish stock
1 quart white mussels
2 shallots, peeled and chopped
11 oz. shelled pink shrimp
11 oz. white mushrooms
2/3 cup liquid *crème fraîche*
3 oz. butter
salt and pepper

La fondue de poireaux sauce dieppoise

Simpler to prepare than a true *sauce normande*, sauce *à la dieppoise* is also made with vegetables.

1- In a pot combine the mussels, 1 3/4 oz. of the white wine, and the *bouquet garni*. Cook 5 minutes to open the mussels. Remove from heat. Drain the mussels and remove them from their shells. Strain and set aside the cooking juices at room temperature.

2- Wash and slice the leeks. Peel and slice the shallots.
Cook the bacon strips over high heat without added fat. When they begin to brown, add the leeks and shallots. Cook, stirring, over low heat for 10 minutes without allowing them to take on much color.

3- Add the mushrooms, the rest of the white wine, and the shrimp. Add salt, pepper, and the ground nutmeg. Simmer over very low heat for about 10 minutes, stirring occasionally.

4- When the leeks are completely softened, add the *crème fraîche*, and the mussels with their cooking juices. Cook 10 minutes more and remove from heat.

5- Serve the leeks as a side dish with grilled fish, or with potatoes in their jackets, or plain as a first course.
You may also serve this dish as a *gratin*, or add eggs and cook it in a pastry shell like a *quiche*.

Serves 6
Preparation : 35 minutes
Cooking time : 40 minutes

14 oz. large pink shrimp, peeled
1 quart cultivated mussels
3 large leeks
2 shallots
7 oz. white mushrooms, washed and chopped
7 oz. smoked bacon, cut into strips
3 1/2 oz. white wine
3 1/2 oz. liquid *crème fraîche*
1 *bouquet garni*
1 teaspoon ground nutmeg
salt and pepper

The *crêpes* and *galettes* of Brittany

Crêpes are found everywhere, but in Brittany they have the distinctive flavor of buckwheat, brought back by crusaders returning from the Middle East. Once considered « poor man's bread », they are now worth their weight in gold in a region where new *crêperies* with « tasting menus » open each year.

Above
The ritual of *crêpe* making in Bigouden country.

Facing page
This device (called a « rozell » in Breton) facilitates spreading the batter in a thin layer. Terminology varies from region to region. In the Côtes-d'Armor area, the *crêpe* is turned with a « latte », which is called a « spannel » in Ille-et-Vilaine.

Picture moors, pasturelands, and stone manor houses with the Montagne Noire looming against the horizon. In a park stand tents and a 650-foot row of « billigs » (special griddles used in preparing *galettes*, which should be both tender and crusty). Expert home cooks have signed up to compete for the most beautiful *crêpe*, while the professionals explain the art of spreading the batter in a single layer, not two as they do elsewhere in Brittany. With tourists and locals elbow to elbow, Gourin pays homage to the *crêpe*.

Buckwheat and wheat
Gourin lies in central Brittany in the Morbihan region. For over ten years, it has been the self-proclaimed capital of Breton *crêpe*-making. The town has four *crêperies* specializing in « tasting menus » and four take-out spots–not many compared with Quimper's twenty-five *crêperies* (for a population of 60,000). But the old hands will assure you that Gourin's *crêperies* have always been famed and that they delivered their products to Paris the morning after VE Day.

There is really no food more universal than the *crêpe*. It goes by the name of « blini », « brick », or « pancake » elsewhere in the world, but the notion of pouring a little batter on a *galet* (griddle, whence the name *galette*), is as old as civilization and is as ubiquitous in China as it is in Limousin. All over France people have *crêpes* sizzling on the griddle on the feast day of Chandeleur. It is a way of celebrating the Presentation of Jesus in the Temple with a dish symbolic of plenty. Even classic French cuisine makes good use of *crêpes* in the form of *aumonières* and *pannequets*. In Brittany, however, the *crêpe* is a different matter altogether; it is a symbol of national identity. Terminology only adds to the confusion. Around Vitré, in the Celtic region, it seems quite straightforward: the *galette* is slightly salty with a buckwheat base, while the *crêpe* is made with white flour and sweetened. But in other areas, such as Finistère and the Côtes-d'Armor, *galettes* made with white flour are on the dessert menu, and buckwheat *crêpes* are a main course. Stendhal attempted to summarize the matter this way: « People in the area of Brittany where the Breton language is spoken live on buckwheat flour *galettes*. » The truth is not so simple. The meaning of words may evolve, but the underlying reality never changes: it is all a balance between buckwheat and white flour, between hard times and prosperity.

Makes 24 *crêpes*
Preparation time : 10 minutes
Resting time : 2 hours (optional)
Cooking time : 45 minutes

1 lb. wheat flour
3 eggs
1 quart, 2 oz. milk
2 3/4 oz. melted lightly salted butter, plus about 3 1/2 oz. additional butter for cooking
7 oz. granulated sugar
juice of 1 lemon

Serves 12
Preparation time : 25 minutes
Resting time : 3 hours
Cooking time : about 45 minutes

14 oz. buckwheat flour
4 1/2 oz. wheat flour
1 quart, 2 oz. milk
1 3/4 oz. butter
pinch of coarse salt
7 oz. lightly salted butter, melted, for cooking
cheese, ham, a variety of sausages, and eggs for toppings

Les crêpes

Traditional *crêpe* batter is used for sweetened dishes. *Crêpes* are best eaten as they are cooked. If this is not possible, stack them on a plate and keep them warm in a double boiler.

1- Prepare the batter. Combine the flour and sugar in a large bowl, and make a well in it with your fingertips.
2- Break the eggs into the well and carefully pour in the milk, stirring with a whisk just until the batter is mixed.
3- Add the lemon juice and melted butter, whisking very lightly. Let the batter stand 2 hours at room temperature.
4- Heat a large non-stick pan with a small amount of butter. Pour a small ladleful of the batter into the melted butter, spread the batter out and cook the *crêpe* over medium heat for 3 minutes.
5- When it is browned, turn it over carefully with a wooden spatula, and cook the other side for 2 minutes.

Les galettes

Galettes, a Breton specialty, have a buckwheat base and are eaten with savory toppings.

1- Prepare the *galette* batter in the same way you would *crêpe* batter, adding the coarse salt, and let it rest 3 hours.
2- Roll a small piece of string into the shape of a cork and attach it to the end of a fork with a thread. Soak the string in melted butter and use it to grease the pan.
3- When the butter smokes, pour a small ladleful of batter into the pan and spread it out. Cook 2 minutes, then carefully flip the *galette* over without breaking it. (Careful! *Galettes* are more fragile than *crêpes*.)
4- Add the filling(s) of your choice, then fold the edges inward with a spatula. Leave the *galette* in the pan for another 2 minutes, then turn it over again. Cook an additional 2 minutes and slide it directly onto a serving plate. Just before serving, rub a little piece of cold, lightly salted butter over the top of the crusty *galette*.

Facing page
A row of cast iron griddles (called « billig » in Breton) on which a crêpe maker has just poured a thin layer of batter. The challenge is to spread it out evenly with a single sweep.

Far left
Once the crêpe has been turned, the last step is to rub it with a piece of cool butter.

Near left
It was a short step from crêpes to crêpes dentelles. Jacques Thorel, one of Brittany's greatest chefs, was the innovator.

The wheat of the infidel

The story begins when the crusaders returned home, bringing back with them buckwheat, also known as « black wheat.» The plant, which is related to sorrel, bears charming white flowers and produces a seed whose shape resembles that of a beech tree. Its dark color, as well as its origin in time of war against the swarthy infidel, earned it the name *sarracenus*, whence the word *sarrasin*. Long cultivated in China, Japan, Russia, and throughout the Middle East, it became prevalent in the seventeenth century in France's most impoverished regions, the Massif Central and Brittany. Buckwheat could thrive in soil too poor for wheat; it flourished in humid conditions and was not subject to taxes. Breton farmers became accustomed to selling the little wheat flour they were able to produce at market, while keeping the buckwheat harvest for themselves.

Bread made from buckwheat does not rise well, so *crêpes*, which did not require leavening, became the bread of the poor. The mistress of the house usually chose Friday, a fast day, to labor over her stove to prepare the « daily bread » for the week ahead. If she couldn't make a *kig-ha farz*, a sort of stew based on buckwheat flour from the Léonard region, the family would soak the increasingly stale *galettes*, day after day, in gruel, milk, or meat broth.

As buckwheat became rooted and cherished in Brittany's cooking, this interloper from distant lands came to be perceived as specifically Breton. « Buckwheat from Brittany can be picked out from a thousand other varieties. It has a smaller, silver gray seed, with rounded edges, » explains Catherine Cateline, who operates the Moulin de la Fatigue in Vitré with her husband. This is a place where the miller works the old-fashioned way and is proud that nothing has changed. There are granite millstones and rotating drums to process the flour. « We certainly went through some difficult times. Thirty years ago, buckwheat was out of fashion. Now we have a hard time keeping up with demand. »

This is the ceaseless lament of the peninsula's forty millers, who cannot persuade farmers to reintroduce buckwheat as a crop. By current standards, buckwheat yields are low and its cultivation does not lend itself to mechanization. In contrast to his forbears, today's Breton farmer cannot hope to make a living from buckwheat alone without other sources of income. As a result, France–and Brittany, its principal buckwheat grower–produce only ten percent of what it consumes, and imports the balance. History has its revenge, and a bushel of buckwheat is now more costly than wheat flour.

Masters of the « billig »

« After the Friday market in Quimperlé, all the grandmothers stop by Ty-Gwechall to order a plain crêpe au beurre, *the kind they used to make at home. »*

Buckwheat, an almost nutritionally complete cereal product, is very popular these days. The market for Breton *crêpes* is expanding exponentially. There are now 4,800 *crêperies* in France, with 2,000 in Brittany alone. In 1972, Louise Le Bars opened the Crêperie du Musée, the second such restaurant in Concarneau. Now the town has almost as many *crêperies* as seagulls. From Bréhat to the Arrée mountains, *crêpe-*

This page, above and below
The *crêpe* festival held in Gourin, a town in Brittany's interior. Elegantly turned-out beauties, nostalgic locals, tourists, and young people come to join the party.

Facing page
A traditional Breton coiffe. Was it the inspiration for *crêpes dentelles?*

ries de dégustation, featuring tasting menus, with a décor of lace curtains, weathered paneling, and cider bowls, are an integral part of the Brittany of popular imagination. They may have originally opened for the tourist trade, but now they also cater to the locals, who come as families to rediscover flavors that disappeared with their grandmothers.

The knack for making *crêpes*, which traditionally passed from mother to daughter, is almost lost. In peak summer season, expert traditional *crêpe* makers are so scarce that they are worth their weight in gold. More and more training programs are available for aspiring cooks. Treblec, a miller in Maure-de-Bretagne, has actually proposed the creation of a school for training master *crêpe*-makers, an idea that has been taken up by several regional authorities.

Crêpes have gone through an evolution as a result. Some *crêperies*, such as Ty-Gwechell in Quimperlé, have hired a chef to work beside their traditional *crêpe* maker. *Crêpes* have become a jumping off point for innovation. *Crêpes* topped with warm oysters, perch filets, tuna diced with seasoned artichokes, or seaweed jostle on the menu with the old standby *crêpe complète*, with its ham, egg, and cheese.

Some chefs go even farther and view the *crêpe* as simply a base for their creations, recalling the time when they existed just to add a little substance to broth. Guy Guilloux, the innovative chef of Taupinière near Pont-Aven, has introduced the *crêpe* into his sophisticated cuisine; a ribbon of honey and pieces of *pain d'épice* surround the buckwheat *crêpes* that he uses instead of *mille-feuille* pastry in his *foie gras* presentation. Should we take offense at this apparent disregard for tradition,

which turns a dish formerly consumed out of necessity into a luxury? Not necessarily.

At the tables of the great

The *crêpe* has been weaving its own golden legend for a very long time. The story goes that the young duchess Anne of Brittany was on an outing in the forest one day in 1490. Seeking refuge from a sudden storm, she and her retinue took shelter in a woodcutter's cottage. To feed them, the daughter of the house prepared plenty of *galettes* from buckwheat, all she had to offer. They were an instant sensation. Anne, who first married Charles VIII and later Louis XII, introduced this dish from her homeland to the court. The *crêpe* of humble origins found itself on the table of kings.

The Breton middle class began using wheat, the rich

> « *One day the oldest girl in the family would get up from the table to help in the kitchen so her mother could sit down and eat. That's how she got the knack of* crêpe *making.* »

man's grain, as soon as they had the means to do so. At the end of the nineteenth century, *crêpes* took on a new guise in Quimper: they were transformed into lace. Marie-Catherine Cornic, known as « Katell », invented a way to make extraordinarily thin *crêpes* that she then rolled with the end of a knife. Within a few years, her recipe became famous, and her lacy *crêpes* turned up in Paris and all over Europe. Curnonsky relished them, pronouncing them « heavenly.» *Crêpes dentelles* now accompanied the champagne and ice cream served at the most elegant tables.

Production of *crêpes dentelles* became industrialized and soon they were made all over Brittany, and even beyond. One of the finest producers, located in Nantes, was official supplier to the Élysée Palace and Matignon until the owner retired. His successor, Patrick Collin, manager of the Quimper-Stivell bakeries, decided to stay true to tradition « because we love the craftsmanship involved, and also because we are located in Locmaria, Quimper's historic district. » A famous faience factory is located just next door. There is a satisfying justice in the return of this jewel of Breton *crêpe* making to the heart of the old city.

Les pannequets au fromage

Makes 12 *pannequets*
Preparation time : 30 minutes
Resting time : 2 hours (optional)
Cooking time : 45 minutes

9 oz. wheat flour
2 eggs
17 oz. milk
1 1/2 oz. lightly salted butter, plus 1 1/2 oz. additional for cooking

For the fillings
10 1/2 oz. *béchamel* sauce
3 1/2 oz. grated cheese
5 1/2 oz. Roquefort cheese
salt and pepper

Pannequets are *crêpes* rolled up like little packages or filled and folded into quarters. They may be accompanied by meat and *béchamel* sauce, or by honey or a fruit compote. For sweet *pannequets*, replace the *béchamel* with pastry cream and the grated cheese with dried fruit. Of course, you would not add sugar to batter for *crêpes* intended for savory *pannequets*.

1- Put the flour in a large bowl and make a well in it with your fingertips. Break the eggs into the well and add the milk slowly, stirring with a whisk until the ingredients are just blended.
2- Add the melted butter, whisking gently.
3- Heat a large non-stick pan and grease with a small amount of butter. Pour a small ladleful of batter into the warm butter, spread the batter out and cook 3 minutes over medium heat. When the bottom is browned, turn the *crêpe* over carefully with a spatula and cook on the other side for 2 minutes.
4- Lay the *crêpes* out on a work surface. Season them with *béchamel*, grated cheese, and pieces of Roquefort cheese. Add salt and pepper to taste and fold in the edges of the *crêpes* to make little packets.
Arrange them in a large earthenware-baking dish and bake them in a preheated 340° oven for 15 minutes.

Jacques Thorel's *crêpes dentelles*

Makes 12 *crêpes*
Preparation time : 30 minutes
Resting time : overnight
Cooking time : 2 1/2 hours

9 oz. wheat flour
1 tablespoon buckwheat flour
pinch of salt
4 1/2 oz. granulated sugar
2 eggs
17 oz. whole milk
3 1/2 oz. lightly salted butter, plus 3 1/2 oz. for cooking
1 3/4 oz. confectioners' sugar

This is a very old Breton recipe, revived by Jacques Thorel, the two Michelin star chef of his restaurant L'Auberge bretonne in La Roche-Bernard near Saint-Nazaire. These crunchy, brittle *crêpes* are delicious at the end of a meal with a big glass of cider or some raspberry liqueur from Plougastel-Daoulas.

1- Prepare the batter as you would for traditional *crêpes* and let it rest at room temperature overnight.
2- Cook the *crêpes*, making them as thin as possible. Roll them gently without crushing them flat. Bend the ends in to seal them and arrange the *crêpes* on a large baking sheet.
3- Preheat the oven to its lowest setting. Sprinkle the *crêpes* with powdered sugar and place them in the oven. Let them dry and caramelize for about 2 hours, watching them carefully to prevent burning.

Les crêpes légères à la cannelle et au miel caramélisé

These *crêpes* are delicious with hot chocolate. Instead of using ground cinnamon, you may flavor the *crêpes* with cocoa, instant coffee, vanilla extract, or lemon juice.

1- Prepare the batter: put the flour, salt, cinnamon, and sugar in a large bowl. Make a well in the dry ingredients with your fingertips.
2- Open the vanilla bean and scrape out the contents to flavor the cold milk. Break the eggs into the well and gently pour in the vanilla-flavored milk, stirring with a whisk until the ingredients are just blended. Pour in the melted butter and whisk gently. Let the batter rest for 20 minutes.
3- Cook the *crêpes* in the usual way and keep them warm.
4- When you are ready to serve the *crêpes*, warm the honey and cinnamon stick together in a small pot. When the honey becomes foamy and golden, remove from heat. Pour the caramelized honey over the warm *crêpes* and serve immediately.

Makes 12 *crêpes*
Preparation time : 10 minutes
Resting time : 20 minutes
Cooking time : 30 minutes

9 oz. flour
3 eggs
1 quart, 8 oz. milk
1 3/4 oz. lightly salted butter, plus 3 1/2 oz. for cooking
pinch of salt
1 teaspoon granulated sugar
3 teaspoons ground cinnamon
1 cinnamon stick
1 vanilla bean
3 1/2 oz. liquid Gâtinais honey

the northwest

Tarte aux pommes in Normandy

The fragrance of apple tarts brings back the flavors of childhood and Sunday family gatherings. Apple pastries are made everywhere, but it is in Normandy that they attain true greatness. Cream, butter, and heirloom apples are in their element in this countryside of spotted cows and lanes winding between hedgerows.

Above
Black and white cows rest in the shade of an apple tree. Together, the animals and trees create their own typically Norman ecosystem. Translated into culinary terms, it corresponds to the marriage of cream and apples in a *tarte aux pommes* with cream.

Facing page
Harvesting apples, a local treasure, in the Calvados region.

People eat « their very own » apple tarts daily in Japan, Saudi Arabia, and China. Gaston Lenôtre, who was born on a farm in the Pays d'Auge, began his career as an apprentice pastry chef and grew up to become an ambassador of the delicacies of France and the emperor of restaurateurs everywhere, but he never forgot the *tarte aux pommes* of his native Normandy. Paying homage to his mother, who cooked for the Rothschilds, he christened his version the « Eléonore » and always listed it on his menu. « Beginning Friday night, » he recounts in *Le Petit Castelot gourmand*, « I had to peel and cube entire crates of apples. I filled up huge stoneware pots like the ones used for salting butter: a layer of apples, a few spoonfuls of sugar and vanilla, another layer of apples and so on. The next morning, when the three-level coal-burning oven reached the right temperature, I had to load the baking racks and put the biggest tarts in the back and the smaller ones in front… » The process was already professional, but the memories are very personal, taking one back to childhood.

Childhood memories

The thought of a *tarte aux pommes* evokes the appealing warmth of the oven, the bustle of mothers and grandmothers, the feeling of hands in the flour. It makes us think about eager children, snacks in the garden, and desserts shared around the family table. Michel Bruneau, whose restaurant La Bourride is now regarded as one of the best in Caen, pays homage to the women who gave his Thursdays the sweet tang of fruit and sugar. Not content with offering a dessert assortment where a thick *tarte aux pommes* is flanked by *sorbets*, *douillons*, and other apple delicacies, he has recently published a book devoted to the desserts of Normandy. The tart, in all its variations, reigns supreme. « There were never any cookies in our knapsacks, » he recalls. « We always got homemade treats baked by my grandmother and godmother. I'm told that I climbed up on a stool to see what was cooking in the oven. »

> « You have to admit that a tarte aux pommes, still warm from the oven, is a true wonder, » writes Michel Bruneau.

The apple tart is certainly one of the oldest and best loved desserts in the world. It can be found in its countless variations in Brie, the Alps, Provence, and Sologne, the home of the legendary Tatin sisters. It is a tart you can find everywhere, but Normandy does

La tarte aux pommes à la normande

Tarte normande is a classic apple tart, flambéed with Calvados, and served with *crème fraîche*. The apples are sometimes poached in syrup before being arranged on the pastry.

1- First make the pastry: mix the butter and sugar with a spatula, then add the eggs and mix together with your fingertips. Add the flour all at once and continue to mix with your fingertips until the dough is creamy and smooth. Wrap it in a towel and place it in the refrigerator for 40 minutes to firm.

2- Peel and core the apples. Cut a third of them up into small pieces and cook them down into a compote in a pot with 1 ounce of the sugar and the butter, stirring. Slice the remaining apples in quarters. Preheat the oven to 350°.

3- Press the dough into a tart pan. Pour the compote on top. Carefully lay the quartered apples on top in a rosette pattern, and sprinkle them with the rest of the sugar. Bake the tart for 30 minutes.

4- When the tart is cooked, remove it from the oven. Warm the Calvados in a small pot and light it carefully, using a long match. Immediately pour the flaming Calvados over the apple tart to flambé it. Let the tart stand a few minutes before cutting it. Serve it very hot, topped with a dollop of *crème fraîche*.

Serves 6
Preparation time : 1 hour
Resting time : 40 minutes
Cooking time : 45 minutes

For the pastry
10 1/2 oz. flour
4 1/2 oz. granulated sugar
4 1/2 oz. softened butter
2 eggs

For the topping
3 lbs., 5 oz. of apples (Golden Delicious or *reinettes*)
2 oz. granulated sugar
2 3/4 oz. butter
7 oz. *crème fraîche*
3 1/2 oz. Calvados

La tarte qui cuit deux fois

In this recipe, the tart shell is baked unfilled. The apples, cooked separately, are added later.

1- First make the pastry: mix the butter and sugar with a spatula, then add the eggs and mix together with your fingertips. Add the flour all at once and continue to mix with your fingertips until the dough becomes creamy and smooth. Wrap it in a towel and put it into the refrigerator for 40 minutes to firm.

2- Press the dough into a tart pan; fill the tart shell with dry beans and bake in a preheated 350° oven for 30 minutes.

3- Peel and core the apples. Cut into quarters. Mix the sugar with 16 oz. water and bring to a boil. Immerse the apple quarters in the boiling syrup for 5 minutes, then drain them on a plate. Beat the egg yolks with the *crème fraîche* in a bowl.

4- When the pastry shell is cooked, take it out of the oven and remove the dried beans. Arrange the apple quarters on the cooked tart shell and cover it with the *crème fraîche*-egg mixture. Put the tart back in the oven at 300° for 10 minutes to brown.

5- When the apple quarters are cooked and the custard is firm, remove the tart from the oven. Let it cool and sprinkle with confectioners' sugar before serving.

Serves 6
Preparation time : 1 hour
Resting time : 40 minutes
Cooking time : 45 minutes

For the pastry
10 1/2 oz. flour
4 1/2 oz. granulated sugar
4 1/2 oz. softened butter
2 eggs
18 oz. dried beans to weight down the raw pastry shell

For the topping
3 lbs., 5 oz. Golden Delicious apples
10 1/2 oz. granulated sugar
1 3/4 oz. liquid *crème fraîche*
2 egg yolks
1 tablespoons confectioners' sugar

lay its own special claim to this dessert. « There's a special kind of openhanded generosity in Normandy, » Michel Bruneau explains. « The region is sometimes criticized for adding butter, cream, and sugar with a heavy hand, but for a *tarte aux pommes*, that's a requirement. You absolutely cannot skimp. And then there's the exceptional quality of the products. After all, this is the only region of France where an AOC (Government Certification of Origin) is awarded to butter and cream. » Seen from this point of view, a *tarte aux pommes* has a steadfast kinship with the landscape of the Pays d'Auge valley and the lanes bordered by hedgerows that wind through the Pays de Caux.

Pomme de reinette and *pomme d'api*

« Man has fashioned our landscape. We are one with the countryside, » says Thierry Defrièches. He is the son, grandson, and great grandson of cider makers, producing Père Jules ciders and Calvados in Saint-Désir-de-Lisieux. He has seen people working with apples for as long as he can remember.

« I am struggling to preserve the old-fashioned tall apple trees, » he explains, « because that is the only way that you can pasture cows around them. Cows help maintain the orchard, and provide the fertilizer it needs. The hedges mark boundaries and also cut the wind, so in springtime they protect the blossoms from late frosts. It all makes sense. »

Of course, each plot of land lends its own distinct flavor to what it produces. « Even coming from a few yards apart, cream and butter don't taste the same, because the grass the cows eat is not the same, » Thierry Defrièches explains. « The apples you'll find here taste different from the ones you'll get elsewhere, even if they're from nearby Seine-Maritime. » The flavors of different heirloom apples vary also: they are more or less tart or sweet and some have an edge of bitterness. Defrièches recites their names with delight: *cimitière de Blangy, rouge-duret, frequin rouge, Noël des champs* for cider making; *reine des reinettes, Bénédictin, calville,* and *belle de Boskoop* for use in cooking tarts, as well as duck or black sausage.

> « Every cook has her own little secrets at home, her own little tricks of the trade, and none of them are written down. »

To each his own...*tarte normande*

The recipe for *tarte normande* is as familiar as a souvenir postcard. Spread apple compote on short pastry, add coarsely cut apples; cover with a mixture of eggs and cream. « The truth is that there is no official recipe, » states Michel Bruneau. « Some cooks use a puff pastry, others a pie dough. You can cook the apples in advance, or use them raw. You can sprinkle the tart with sugar or cover it with meringue, flambé it with Calvados or serve it as is. » And don't forget the little pitcher of cream for the finale. The *tarte normande* is a strategic alliance of hot and cold, soft and crunchy, a celebration in itself.

Les tartelettes fines aux pommes râpées

These little apple tarts are quickly prepared, and come out of the oven deliciously thin and crunchy.

Serves 6
Preparation time : 25 minutes
Cooking time : 35 minutes

1 roll of puff pastry
4 green apples
3 1/2 oz. softened butter
3 1/2 oz. brown sugar
juice of 1 lemon
2 vanilla beans

1- Cut out 6 rounds of dough, each about 3 1/2-inches in diameter, using a cutter (an inverted bowl for example).
Peel and core the apples. Grate them coarsely in a food processor and mix them with the lemon juice. Preheat the oven to 340°.
2- Arrange the pastry rounds on a piece of grease-proof paper and place them on a large tray or pastry rack. Mound equal amounts of the grated apples onto the pastry rounds and sprinkle them with the brown sugar.
3- Open the vanilla beans and scrape out their contents. Mix the vanilla seeds with the butter. Put a piece of vanilla-flavored butter on top of each tart.
4- Bake the tarts 35 minutes. Half way through the cooking time, press down the apple mixture into the pastry with the tip of a fork. The tarts are done when they are brown and lightly caramelized. Remove them from the oven and cool slightly before serving.

Les casse-museau

In Brie, they cook whole apples inside a pastry covering. It is traditional to replace the apple in one of the *casse museau* with an onion. The unlucky person who bites into that one might break a tooth...or a muzzle!

Serves 6
Preparation time : 20 minutes
Resting time : 10 minutes
Cooking time : 30 minutes

6 apples
1 3/4 oz. granulated sugar
6 tablespoons apple jelly
2 oz. butter

For the pastry
17 1/2 oz. flour
8 3/4 oz. butter
1 cup warm water
1 egg yolk for the glaze

1- Mix the flour and softened butter in a large bowl. Add warm water little by little, while mixing the dough with your fingertips. When the pastry is thoroughly blended, wrap it in a dishtowel and let it rest 10 minutes in the refrigerator.
2- Wash and core the apples, but do not peel them.
3- Preheat the oven to 350°. Roll out the pastry and cut into 6 pieces. Place an apple on each piece, fill the inside of the fruit with jelly and top each with a small piece of butter. Fold the pastry up to enclose the apples, retaining their shape.
4- Brush each apple pastry with egg yolk and bake 30 minutes at 350°. 5 minutes before the end of the cooking time, sprinkle them with sugar and return them to the oven to brown. Remove the *casse-museau* from the oven and allow to cool before serving.

Brittany

Le kig-ha farz

Serves 6

Preparation time : 40 minutes

Cooking time : 2 hours 30 minutes

2 lbs., 2 oz. stewing beef
2 lbs., 2 oz. lean bacon
1 *bouquet garni*
6 carrots
2 large leeks
5 turnips
1/2 white cabbage
1 large rutabaga
sea salt, peppercorns

For the *farz*
17 1/2 oz. buckwheat flour
1 tablespoon salt
1 egg
6 3/4 oz. *crème fraîche*
2 1/2 oz. granulated sugar
8 1/2 oz. milk
3 1/2 oz. prunes
1 3/4 oz. raisins

1- Peel and wash the vegetables. Put them whole in a large pot and cover with water. Add the beef, a handful of coarse salt, a tablespoon of peppercorns, the bacon, and the *bouquet garni* and simmer over low heat for 21/2 hours, skimming occasionally.
2- Prepare the *farz*. Work the flour, sugar, salt, egg, milk, and *crème fraîche* together with a spatula. Add the prunes and raisins.
3- Turn the *farz* into a cloth bag, filling it 3/4 full to allow the mixture to expand as it cooks. Close the sack with a string and tie the end of the string to the pot's handle. Immerse the bag in the meat and vegetable broth. If you do not have a bag, you may substitute a dishtowel tied with kitchen string.
4- When the meat is cooked, drain it and put it on a serving plate. Arrange the bacon and vegetables around the meat. Drain the *farz* and roll the bag on a flat surface to break it up. Arrange the pieces around the meat and vegetables. Sprinkle with a small amount of broth and serve.

L'artichaut à la bretonne

Serves 6

Preparation time : 20 minutes

Cooking time : 1 hour

6 artichoke bottoms
1 large onion
12 oz. strips lightly salted bacon
1/2 bottle of cider
3 1/2 oz. butter
salt and pepper

1- Peel and chop the onion.
2- Melt 1 3/4 oz. of the butter in a pot; add the bacon, onion, and artichoke bottoms. Season with salt and pepper and cover with cider. Cook, stirring, over low heat for 1 hour.
3- When you are ready to serve, drain the artichokes and arrange them on a serving platter or directly on plates. Add remaining butter to the sauce and whisk to incorporate.
4- Remove from heat, correct the seasoning and cover the artichokes with the cider sauce.

La soupe au blé noir

Serves 6

Preparation time : 30 minutes

Cooking time : approximately 1 hour

8 3/4 oz. smoked pork belly, cut into strips
8 3/4 oz. buckwheat flour
2 quarts, 10 oz. water
1 *bouquet garni*
6 slices of bread
5 1/4 oz. lightly salted butter

1- Cook the pork strips in 2 1/2 oz. butter over low heat until the pork is lightly browned; do not allow the butter to burn. Add the flour and cook, stirring, 5 minutes.
2- Pour in the cold water and bring to a boil. Add the *bouquet garni* and cook over low heat for 1 hour, stirring often to prevent the soup from sticking.
3- Cut the bread into large pieces. Melt the remaining butter in a pot. Toss the croutons in the butter over high heat, turning them so that they brown on all sides.
4- Correct the seasoning of the soup before serving it very hot in small bowls, sprinkled with the browned croutons.

Le kouing amann

Serves 6

Preparation time : 15 minutes

Cooking time : 30 minutes

4 1/2 oz. flour
8 3/4 oz. dough for sourdough country style bread
8 3/4 oz. softened lightly salted butter, plus 3/4 oz for the mold
10 1/2 oz. granulated sugar
1 egg

1- Preheat the oven to 350°. Combine all the ingredients (except for 1 3/4 oz of the sugar) in a large bowl. Mix with your fingertips.
2- Butter a mold 4 1/2-inches in diameter and spread the dough on the bottom.
3- Sprinkle the remaining sugar on top and bake the *kouing amann* 30 minutes. Remove the cake from the oven, and let it cool slightly before serving.

Le far aux pruneaux

Serves 6

Preparation time : 20 minutes

Cooking time : 1 hour

8 3/4 oz. flour
6 1/2 oz. granulated sugar
3 1/2 oz.raisins
4 1/4 oz. prunes
2 tablespoons rum
1 quart, 2 oz. milk
6 eggs
1 3/4 oz. butter for the mold

1- Preheat the oven to 340°. Mix the eggs with the sugar, whisking vigorously. Carefully add the flour, stir to combine, and add the rum.
2- Pour in the cold milk, stirring continuously. The batter should be liquid and creamy.
3- Butter a gratin dish, and fill with the batter. Add the raisins and unpitted prunes, and bake 1 hour. The *far* is ready when it is browned on top. Let it cool and refrigerate before serving.

Normandy

L'omelette de la mère Poulard

a specialty of Mont-Saint-Michel

Serves 6
Preparation time : 10 minutes
Cooking time : 10 minutes

18 eggs
6 tablespoons *crème fraîche*
4 1/4 oz. lightly salted butter
salt and pepper

1- Separate the egg yolks from the whites. Beat the whites in a large bowl until they form firm peaks. Beat the yolks three at a time with a fork and set them aside in ramekins.
2- Melt 3/4 ounce butter in a pan. When it sizzles, pour in three beaten yolks and stir them in the melted butter with a spatula.
3- Add salt and pepper to taste. When the yolks begin to coagulate, add 1 tablespoon of *crème fraîche* and 2 large spoonfuls of beaten egg whites to the middle of the pan. Lower the heat, season with additional salt and pepper, then fold in the edges of the *omelette*, rolling it gently.
4- Cook the *omelette* 2 minutes. Separate it with a spatula from the side of the pan, slide it onto a plate and keep warm. Repeat for remaining *omelettes*, being careful to wipe the pan with absorbent paper between cooking each one.

Le poulet vallée d'Auge

Serves 6
Preparation time : 20 minutes
Cooking time : 1 hour 10 minutes

1 good farm-raised chicken, cut into 6 pieces
4 tablespoons Calvados
5 1/4 oz. *crème fraîche*
2 3/4 oz. butter
3 shallots
10 1/2 oz. small white mushrooms
10 1/2 oz. *mousserons* (field mushrooms)
1 egg yolk
salt and pepper

1- Peel and finely slice the shallots and wash the mushrooms carefully. Melt the butter in a pan and cook the chicken pieces, well seasoned with salt and pepper, briefly over high heat without letting them brown. Add the sliced shallots and whole white mushrooms. Pour over 1 cup water and simmer over low heat for 1 hour.
2- When the chicken is done, flambé the pieces in Calvados and arrange them on a serving platter.
3- Add the *crème fraîche* and *mousserons* to the cooking juices in the pan and cook 10 minutes over low heat. Remove from heat and thicken the sauce by whisking in the egg yolk. Cover the chicken with the *vallée d'Auge* Calvados and cream sauce and serve.

Les maquereaux au vin blanc ou au cidre

Serves 6
Preparation time : 20 minutes
Resting time : 10 minutes
Cooking time : 10 minutes

6 mackerel, prepared by your fishmonger
1 large onion
1 shallot
1 carrot
1 *bouquet garni*
3/4 bottle of good white wine or good dry cider
1 3/4 oz. butter for greasing the baking dish
salt and pepper

1- Chop the onion and shallot. Cut the carrot into slivers.
2- Butter a large earthenware baking dish. Rinse the mackerel under cool water, then lay them whole in the platter. Add the carrot strips, the *bouquet garni*, and the chopped onion and shallots. Season with salt and pepper. Preheat the oven to 320°.
3- Bring the wine or cider to a boil. Pour it over the mackerel and their seasoning and let the preparation marinate for 10 minutes. Bake for 10 minutes.
4- Remove the baking dish from the oven and let it cool. The mackerel may be eaten cold as a first course with slices of bread and salted butter, but they may also be enjoyed warm as a main dish accompanied by steamed potatoes which can be mashed into the savory cooking juices.

Les côtes de veau à la normande

Serves 6
Preparation time : 20 minutes
Cooking time : 20 minutes

6 veal scallops
2 3/4 oz. butter
17 oz. *crème fraîche*
1 3/4 oz. Calvados
6 3/4 oz. dry cider
2 shallots
18 oz. white mushrooms
salt and pepper

1- Peel and slice the shallots. Wash and mince the mushrooms. Melt the butter over low heat in a large skillet. When it foams, cook the veal scallops quickly, and add the sliced shallots and minced mushrooms.
2- Season the veal scallops with salt and pepper and turn them over in the pan. Pour off the grease from the skillet and flambé the scallops in the Calvados. Then add the cider to the skillet.
3- Reduce the cider by half and add the *crème fraîche*. Continue to baste the veal scallops with the cooking juices. When the *sauce normande* takes on a creamy consistency, taste it and correct the seasoning. Serve the veal scallops covered with the sauce and the mushrooms. This recipe is delicious accompanied by purees of Golden Delicious apples and potatoes.

Picture the North Sea stretching all the way to Holland, Paris, a crossroads of the world, Alsace, where the great civilizations of the East have mingled. The cooking of the Northeast symbolizes French cuisine in its entirety, powerful in its own right, but open to influences from all sides. This is a cuisine that has long since established an unassailable reputation.

Moules-frites in the North

Along the coasts of Flanders and Picardie, from Artois and all the way to Belgium, the thought of *moules-frites* evokes recollections of foggy vacation days and snug little restaurant hideaways. It's a perfectly simple dish, almost a culinary oddity, which great Parisian chefs find just as intriguing as fast food aficionados.

Above
Mussels are done when their shells open by themselves. A moment before, they make the cooking pot's cover do a little dance.

Facing page, above
On the Côte d'Opale, vacations have the flavor of spindrift and ocean mists. Bathing cabanas (the ones shown here are in Wimereux) allow you to enjoy a little home away from home by the beach.

Facing page, below
Service is fast and efficient in the brasserie Aux moules, Lille's temple of moules-frites, where the heap of discarded shells just gets higher and higher during the open air festival.

Every weekend before the first Monday in September, the restaurant Aux Moules, Lille's temple of *moules-frites*, hires a few extra employees. Their job is to stand guard day and night over an elegant construction made from heaps of shells, which looms like a steely gray pyramid in one corner of the terrace. The tradition of piling the shells of tons of mussels consumed during the huge open air market started here in 1930 with special municipal authorization, and it is now observed all over the city. It began as the solution to a practical problem, disposal of the debris that accumulated in restaurants over a short period of time during the festival. The manager had the inspiration to request permission to pile them on the sidewalk. Other restaurants followed suit, and it was not long before a rumor spread about a mysterious competition for the biggest pile of mussel shells. This competition was a figment of the popular imagination, but the notion is significant in itself. « I wonder if the pile of shells unconsciously bring to mind the slag heaps you see here and there in

the countryside? » ventures Patricia Dariosecq who orchestrates the event at the *brasserie*.

A truly Flemish dish

A few kilometers from metropolitan Lille, Chris Marquet serves golden, crisp fries in his village inn in Godewaersvelde in the Flemish heartland. Fries are ubiquitous here. They accompany *coq à la bière*, *potjevfleisch*, tasty grilled sausages and, of course, mussels. In village squares, traveling *friteries* are set up every year, flaunting the crest of Flanders, a yellow lion rampant on a black ground. Are *frites* Belgian or French? Chris rejects the underlying premise of the question. « They're Flemish, and that's all there is to it. »

« Moules-frites *here are like* steak-frites *in other parts of France, an elemental dish.* »

After studying Flemish cuisine for over twenty years, the historian Jacques Messiant asserts, « Flanders discovered the potato about 100 years before Parmentier promoted the tuber throughout the rest of France at the end of the eighteenth century. » Potatoes had not yet made the transition from the soup pot to the deep fryer. As Bruegel's canvases attest, frying was a very basic cooking method in the region. Small fish, such as sprats or herrings, were plunged into vats of oil or other fat in the town

Les moules marinières
et les pommes de terre frites

Serves 6
Preparation time : 30 minutes
Cooking time : 20 minutes

For the mussels
6 1/2 quarts *bouchot* mussels
5 3/4 oz. butter
3 1/2 oz. white wine
1 onion
4 shallots
1 bunch chopped parsley

For the *frites*
2 lbs., 4 oz. large potatoes
3 3/4 quarts oil or other fat for frying
Guérande salt

Here are the classic recipes for *moules marinières* and *pommes frites*. Belgians use large Belgian or Dutch mussels and sometimes the *zeeland* variety. They use water instead of white wine to open them and add a stalk of celery.

1- Peel and mince the shallots and onion. Wash and coarsely chop the parsley.
2- Prepare the *frites*. Peel the potatoes, trim them flat on 4 sides and cut them into slices 2- to 2 1/2-inches thick. Then cut them into medium-size sticks. Rinse the potato sticks in cold water, drain them and dry them in a clean dishtowel.
3- Place the potatoes in the frying basket and immerse them for 5 minutes in boiling oil or fat. Drain them. Immerse them again in the boiling oil or fat, this time moving them around with a long handled fork, for 6 to 8 minutes.
As soon as the potatoes are crisp and well browned, drain them on a cloth or paper towels and salt them. Keep them warm in the oven while you finish preparing the mussels.
4- While the potatoes are cooking, combine the mussels, butter, white wine, onion, and shallots in a large pot. Cook them over high heat for 10 minutes, stirring vigorously.
5- When the mussels have all opened, sprinkle them with the chopped parsley and place the hot cooking pot directly on the table accompanied by the *frites*.

Les moules marinière infusées
à la verveine d'Alain Passard

Serves 6
Preparation time : 20 minutes
Cooking time : 10 minutes

3 1/4 quarts *bouchot* mussels
1 sprig of fresh lemon verbena (Save 5 leaves for Step 3)
4 shallots
4 1/2 oz. butter
freshly ground pepper

It takes a daring man to replace white wine with an infusion of lemon verbena, but the result is delicious and it marries beautifully with the mussels. This recipe comes from Alain Passard, the Michelin three-star chef of the restaurant L'Arpège in Paris's 7th *arrondissement*.

1- Peel and mince the shallots. Strip the verbena leaves from the stem and wash them.
2- 20 minutes before you are ready to serve, combine the mussels, 2 3/4 oz. of the butter, the minced shallots and the verbena in a large pot. Cook over high heat for 10 minutes, stirring vigorously.
3- When the mussels open, strain the cooking liquid and reduce it slightly. Add 5 verbena leaves and allow them to steep for 5 minutes as you would for an herbal tea.
4- Bring the verbena-flavored cooking liquid to a boil and whisk in the rest of the butter piece by piece. Correct the seasoning. Remove the mussels from their shells, and replace them on the bottom half of the shells. Arrange the mussels on individual plates and serve them covered with the verbena scented juices.

square. One day a cook from Flanders, or Wallonia, or Dunkerque (depending on who is telling the story) found he had run out of fish. He had the idea of cutting potatoes into little sticks to mimic the missing commodity and the *frite* was born!

When preparing *frites* today, connoisseurs unhesitatingly choose the *bintje*, the queen of potato varieties grown in these rich, well-watered fields. They are slightly floury and their flesh is protected by sturdy skin. After being cut up and dried off, they are fried in two steps, first at a lower temperature to cook them through and then at very high heat to give them a crunchy exterior.

Zeeland or *bouchot*?

Mussels have been eaten in Flanders since the Middle Ages, traditionally prepared in their own juices, or with vinegar or white wine. You can tell when mussels are done because the pot's lid begins to rattle. This is a bit of lore that you will hear throughout the region, despite differing methods of harvesting the shellfish.

Near Ostende and Bray-Dunes, everyone insists on the *zeeland* variety. Around the port of Boulogne-sur-Mer, a transit point for mussels imported from all over the world, the be-all and end-all is the local wild

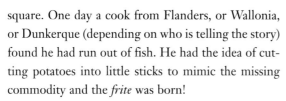

mussel, which has left its mark on the imagination and the economy of this part of the coast.

Twenty years ago, there were still many who made their living gathering shellfish by hand in the early hours of low tide, filling hemp sacks to the brim with little wild mussels, which had to be scrubbed and cleaned one by one. These days, this tiring, time-consuming work is on the wane, but there are still a few die-hards who hold out and continue the practice. They have no difficulty whatsoever selling their harvest, though–people clamor for these mussels.

At the mouth of the Somme, locals have no hesitation in choosing *bouchots*. These mussels grow in bunches on oak stakes, a system that protects them from parasites and sand. *Bouchots* have a lovely bright orange color and an incomparable flavor. For a long time they were confined to the bay of Mont-Saint-Michel and the Vendée region; this form of cultivation had been introduced to the area in the thirteenth century by an Irishman who had been shipwrecked in the bay of l'Aiguillon. In the last twenty years, *bouchots* have become a specialty of Le Crotoy. Cooks here add a bit of cream to their preparation–after all, Normandy is not far away.

How opposites attract

All along the North Sea coast, *moules-frites* have come to symbolize cozy vacations, fishermen's sweaters and laughing gulls, love songs, and visits to local haunts aglow with reddish light. The dish is a kind of rallying point, a shared cultural icon, whether you are camping in the dunes at Ostende or find yourself

As Jacques Brel sang, « Moules-frites are like a crossborder treaty among these lands, Picardie, Belgium, and the Netherlands. »

standing in the windswept streets of Boulogne one autumn evening, gazing at the ferries departing for England.

It is a simple, inexpensive dish, redolent of both land and sea. The astonishing thing is that the two basic ingredients go beautifully together in defiance of good culinary logic. First of all, it is heretical to combine fried and boiled foods, crisp and soft. This is one heresy that continues to spread, however. The *brasserie* Chez Léon, a modest *friterie* established near Brussels' Grand-Place in 1893, has become an institution. Even Alain Passard, one of France's most highly esteemed and innovative chefs, made a pass at *moules-frites* before converting to vegetarianism. He used only *bouchots*, abjured white wine and added his own personal touch, a sprig of fresh verbena. Soon mussels and fries were cooking away on the professional range in the kitchen of a Michelin three-star restaurant. *Moules-frites*–it's a dish that looks very simple, but happily accommodates all the elegant trappings one cares to offer it.

Facing page, left
In the waters around Crotoy, mussels spiral around stakes locally called « bouchots », whence the name for the mussels raised in the area.

Facing page, right
In Ambleteuse near Boulogne-sur-Mer, wild mussels are still harvested by hand. Hugues Sellier, a restaurant owner, collects mussels at low tide all year round.

Above
Returning from the harvest in the Baie de Somme. At low tide, the tractors of the mussel farmers are the only vehicles permitted to enter this carefully preserved desert of sand.

Les fritures de moules et la purée de pommes de terre à la fourchette

Serves 6
Preparation time : 30 minutes
Cooking time : 1 hour

4 1/4 quarts *bouchot* mussels, cooked
marinière style (see page 50)
6 potatoes
2 oz. lightly salted butter
2 3/4 oz. flour
2 eggs
oil for frying
coarse salt and pepper
deep fryer

1- Wash the potatoes and cook them, unpeeled, in the oven at 350° on a bed of coarse salt. When they are done, cut them open and remove the flesh with a small spoon. Mash it with a fork.

2- Remove the mussels from their cooking liquid and drain. Remove them from their shells. Beat the eggs with 2 tablespoons of water in a deep bowl.

3- Dip the mussels, 10 at a time, in the beaten eggs and then in the flour and set them aside on a plate.

4- Heat the oil in the deep fryer. Strain the mussel cooking liquid and reduce it by half. Cook the mussels in 3 batches in the hot oil. Let them brown about 5 minutes, then drain them on absorbent paper.

5- Bring the cooking liquid to a simmer, add the butter and whisk it in without allowing the mixture to boil. Correct the seasoning.

6- Season the fried mussels with salt and pepper and reheat the potato puree in a small pot or in the microwave for 2 minutes. Distribute the puree on the individual plates and pour the reduced, seasoned cooking liquid over. Serve with the fried mussels.

Onion soup in Paris

Soupe à l'oignon is one of the most widespread recipes in France, but Paris has made a specialty of it and re-christened it *gratinée des Halles*. Near the foundations of the church of Saint-Eustache, the soup gives fresh strength nightly to the « the belly of Paris. » Late night partygoers and laborers who begin their work at dawn sit side by side over a bowl of this elixir.

Above
Beneath its golden topping of melted gruyère, onion soup reinvigorates the night owls.

Facing page
The door of the « Pied du Cochon », a restaurant in les Halles in Paris, has no key. The place never closes.

In the neighborhood where Paris' old food market once stood between the lopsided facades of rue Coquillière and the arcades of the rue de Rivoli, the national onion soup is not known as *soupe à l'oignon*, but as *gratinée des Halles*. It is a dish that brings together night laborers who go to bed when the rest of the world is waking up, men about town with collars unbuttoned under their wrinkled tuxedos and ladies of the night in crumpled silk gowns. The wholesale purveyors have been displaced and the gutted neighborhood has been subjected to rather brutal urban renewal. The surviving zinc-topped bars, hand-painted signs, postcards tacked up on walls, opalescent lamps, and lace curtains are treasured like valuable antiques.

Good institutions survive the ravages of urban renewal and changing trends. *Soupe à l'oignon* endures as a time-honored ritual.

Madame Suzanne's bar

There's a crowd every night at Chez Clovis', the Tour de Montlhéry and the Poule au Pot, all smoky bistros with the patina of age that don't open before nightfall. In contrast, the Pied de Cochon shelters four stories of diners and has no locks on its doors because the establishment has never gotten around to closing since Liberation Day.

> « *The tale of the* gratinée *was told in the real heart of Paris—its belly—immortalized by Zola.* »

Jean-François Lecerf, 35 years with the restaurant, wears a tuxedo and a bow tie to greet his guests appropriately, welcoming them in his strong Parisian accent. He has seen all of fashionable Paris at his tables. « I've served a government minister and his bodyguards, a cast of actors, butchers who've finished up their day's work, taxi drivers, hard-drinking students, bums who come in to warm up, the whores and guys who stroll along the rue Saint-Denis, cops and doctors all in one evening, plenty of times. Even Poutine has come to eat here on a private visit. »

La gratinée à l'oignon

1- Peel and cut up the onions. Melt the butter in a sauté pan, add the oil and let them heat together for 1 minute. Cook the onions briefly over high heat. Turn down the heat and cook them 15 minutes over low heat until they color lightly.

2- Sprinkle the flour on top of the onions and pour over the chicken broth. Season with salt and pepper and simmer over low heat for 30 minutes, stirring occasionally.

3- Pour the soup into a tureen or 6 individual bowls and place the toasted slices of *baguette* on top. Add a thick layer of grated cheese and brown the toast under the broiler. Serve piping hot.

Serves 6
Preparation time : 15 minutes
Cooking time : 50 minutes

1/2 baguette, sliced and toasted
6 large onions
18 oz. grated gruyère
3/4 oz. flour
2 3/4 oz. butter
2 tablespoons peanut oil
1 quart, 2 oz. chicken broth
salt and pepper

Les crostinis à la fondue d'oignons rouges caramélisés

This simple, thrifty recipe can be prepared during cocktail hour.

1- Peel and chop the onions. Heat the oil in a frying pan and cook the onions briefly over high heat, then let them brown over low heat for 10 minutes, stirring constantly until they are soft and caramelized. Keep them warm.

2- Toast the bread in the oven. Cover the slices with the caramelized onion and arrange them in one layer in a large earthenware cooking dish.

3- Place a large piece of fresh Parmesan on each bread slice, season with salt and pepper, and put them under the broiler until the cheese is melted. Allow them to cool slightly and serve as an hors d'oeuvre with a good red wine.

Serves 6
Preparation time : 25 minutes
Cooking time : 20 minutes

12 slices crusty country style bread
3 red onions
2 3/4 oz. olive oil
5 1/4 oz. fresh Parmesan cheese
salt and pepper

La tarte à l'oignon gratinée

You can prepare several tarts in advance and serve them to your guests at the end of a summer party as you would onion soup in the cold winter months.

1- Prepare the pastry. Put the flour in a large bowl, add the butter cut up into small pieces, the salt and the egg yolk. Mix together with your fingertips, adding enough water (about 2 oz.) to make the dough smooth. Wrap in a dishtowel and let it rest in the refrigerator for 1 hour.

2- Press the dough into a tart dish, pierce it with a fork and let it rest 10 minutes in the refrigerator.

3- Peel and chop the onions. Melt the butter in a cast iron pan. Cook the onions in the butter briefly over high heat and then cook over low heat for 30 minutes, stirring frequently. Preheat the oven to 340°.

4- Cut the ham slices into small cubes and mix these with the cooked onions. Correct the seasoning, adding salt and pepper to taste.

5- Fill the pastry crust with the onion and ham mixture. Sprinkle the grated cheese on top and bake 35 minutes.

6- Remove the tart from the oven, and season with freshly ground pepper. Serve hot or at room temperature.

Serves 6
Preparation time : 40 minutes
Resting time : 1 hour 10 minutes
Cooking time : 1 hour 5 minutes

For the pastry
8 3/4 oz. flour
1 egg yolk
4 1/2 oz. butter, softened
pinch of salt

For the topping
5 large white onions
3 1/2 oz. butter
5 slices cooked ham
3 1/2 oz. grated cheese
salt and freshly ground pepper

The Poule au Pot retains its original décor. « Madame Suzanne opened this bistro in the 1930s. She managed to hang on to her copper bar top through the Occupation, even though the Germans wanted to requisition it for making shells, » explains Paul Racat, the current owner. « I promised not to change anything. » The tradition continues, and the monumental bar and red leatherette upholstered banquettes still welcome hungry guests who gather for a *soupe à l'oignon* and a carafe of Beaujolais at daybreak.

All the flavors of Paris

The custom goes way back, perhaps to 1135 when this neighborhood was dedicated to supplying the necessities of Parisian tables. For centuries it was the transit point for quarters of beef, vegetables, fruit, and fish by the ton. In the nineteenth century, the market was renovated and expanded, and Les Halles, the largest wholesale market in the world, was built. Zola, awed by the vast array of commodities from all over France, depicted every morning at Les Halles as an epic in his novel *Ventre de Paris*. In later years, photographers led by Doisneau and Willy Ronis helped build the legend.

> « Of course, Paris didn't invent the dish. Every country wedding winds up with a bowl of onion soup at dawn. »

Onion soup has always been part of the picture. Simple to prepare, inexpensive, it sticks to the ribs of people who have been working all night in the cold. It's a shot in the arm like a glass of good mulled wine. The dish has assumed the cocky air of a Parisian street urchin. Gruyère and Emmenthal, which are easy to transport to the city from distant alpine retreats, are the most Parisian of cheeses. Slightly stale leftovers of *baguette*, also « Parisian » (as in *baguette de Paris*), make the best croutons to be found anywhere. A *pot-au-feu* simmering for more prosperous patrons could provide the broth for the soup. In sum, this *gratinée de Paris* has all the flavors of Paris itself.

The nocturnal world

After World War II, the neighborhood around Les Halles teemed with people all night long. « The Blanc family who supplied the restaurant's meat bought the Pied de Cochon, » recalls Jean-François Lecerf. « The restaurant, which was across the street from the market's meat pavilion, served as general headquarters for wholesale butchers, the market's special police force, city employees, students hired as part-time help, knife sharpeners, porters, and small scale dealers. » When the curtains fell on the stages along the *grands boulevards* a short distance away, all roads led to the neighborhood that never slept. Late suppers became high fashion. Poets, artists, ladies of the night, and mere common citizens; it was a cross-section of society with its own timeless charm.

Blood-stained smocks and working men's blue overalls have become rarities in the neighborhood around Les Halles these days. With the advent of trailer trucks and the refrigerated warehouses in Rungis, the wholesalers gave up one after another. Even though they still serve a few bowls of *soupe à l'oignon* at the Mareé de Rungis to go with helpings of *têtes de veau* in the early hours of dawn, things are different now. The market workers are isolated like orphans, separated from their former nocturnal comrades. The atmosphere is not the same.

Back in his stronghold in Les Halles, however, Jean-François Lecerf is adamant: there is not a single *grande école* ball that doesn't wind up over a bowl of *soupe à l'oignon*; a DJ who doesn't come in for something restorative; nor an opening night that isn't celebrated here. There are always some representatives of the working class in attendance: cab drivers, waiters, even politicians after long meetings. They've just switched uniforms.

Facing page, below
The croutons made from Parisian baguettes are ready in the bowls. They are indispensable in giving body to the onion soup.

Facing page, above
A few minutes beneath the grill to brown the gruyère topping to golden perfection.

Above
In the large dining room at the Pied de Cochon around four o'clock in the morning: ladies of the night and laborers whose shifts start at dawn feast elbow to elbow.

Choucroute in Alsace

The notion of pickling cabbage to preserve it during winter months is to be found all over central Europe and probably has its origin in Asia. Choucroute, however, is purely Alsatian; it is the Alsatians who codified the accompaniments to create this heartwarming dish you can still find in Alsace today...just as at the great brasseries of Paris!

Above
At Jenny, the large Alsatian brasserie in Paris, waitresses wear traditional costumes. Choucroute is a dish that unifies the entire eastern part of France.

Facing page
The very pale inner leaves of the cabbage, layered like mille-feuille pastry, are used in making sauerkraut. They are cut into very fine slivers, then salted and fermented in barrels or vats.

About 30 kilometers from Strasbourg, not far from the Entzheim airport, the September fields are a fresh green reminiscent of the stories about finding babies in cabbage patches. This is the countryside where *quintal d'Alsace* grows. Every farm used to plant seeds of this heirloom cabbage variety in one corner of the kitchen garden, but now they also grow hybrids developed by the national agricultural institute. Like the *quintal*, they are members of the mighty cabbage family. « The new varieties haven't lost any of their desirable cooking qualities, and they have the advantage of all maturing at the same time; they keep better, and most importantly, they can be mechanically harvested, » explains Paul Merckling, a consultant with the agricultural commission of the Bas-Rhin.

In the old days, people cut cabbages by hand in the field and « whitened » them on the spot, stripping back the dark green outer leaves down to the stem. This skill is almost forgotten today. The occasional resolute tradi-tionalist may still hack the cabbages from their stems, and de-leaf them one after another, then climb on the tow truck to line the globes up, but the vast majority work from tractors fully equipped with mechanical harvesters.

Whatever the harvesting method, the next step barely varies. The cabbage is cut into fine strips, turned into vats, spread out with forks, and trampled down by foot like newly harvested grapes. Add coarse salt and a wood or cement weight to press the mixture down firmly. The next day, beads of white foam appear on top of the vats; fermentation has begun. This is a process that makes the resulting sauerkraut more akin to yogurt than to wine, as it uses lactic fermentation.

« After being harvested, the cabbage starts squirting, bubbling and flying and ends up higgledy-piggledy outside the doors of the choucroute factory. Does all that make it any less good? In either case, it's not a pretty sight. »

La choucroute

This is the classic recipe for *choucroute* where the cabbage is cooked slowly, flavored by juniper berries and bay leaf.

Serves 6
Preparation time : 30 minutes
Cooking time : 1 hour 30 minutes

3 lbs. uncooked sauerkraut
2 onions
3 garlic cloves
2 oz. goose fat
20 oz. Riesling
2 pig's knuckles
1 lb. 4 oz. salted pork loin or
smoked pork chops
7 oz. smoked bacon
7 oz. salt pork
6 Bratwurst or Knockwurst sausages
6 Strasbourg or Frankfurter sausages
12 potatoes
2 bay leaves
2 cloves
10 juniper berries
10 peppercorns
salt

1- Rinse the sauerkraut in cold water several times and drain well. Peel the garlic and onions, chop them, and simmer them in the goose fat in a large pot. Pour over the wine, add half the sauerkraut, the cloves, the bay leaves, the juniper berries, and the peppercorns. Salt lightly and place the pig's knuckles, the bacon, and the pork loin on top, then cover with the remaining sauerkraut.
Cover the pot and simmer over low heat for 1 1/2 hours.
2- Peel the potatoes and cook them in boiling salted water for 30 minutes.
3- 20 minutes before the sauerkraut is ready, pierce the sausages several times with a fork and poach them in a pan of just simmering water.
4- Put the sauerkraut in a heated deep platter, and arrange the drained sausages and potatoes on top. Serve immediately with a good Riesling and a pot of hot mustard.

Is *choucroute* Asian?

Is Alsatian sauerkraut's reputation entirely attributable to local *expertise*? Only in part. This method of fermentation is widespread in most of the world with minor variations. You will encounter it not only in Germany, but also all over central Europe, Russia, and even China. We are told that the builders of the Great Wall ate fermented cabbage. Sailors had learned from Captain Cook's experiment that loading a few barrels of sauerkraut on board prevented scurvy. « Originally, like smoking and salting, fermentation permitted the preservation of local products, » explains Roland Oberlé, a historian. « In Alsace, they fermented turnips and even beans. »

Opinions diverge on sauerkraut's origins, however. In Roland Oberlé's view, the art of pickling cabbage came straight from China via the silk routes or the voyages of Marco Polo. Dr. Thran Ki advances the theory that central Asian nomads mastered of the art of pickling in his book, *Le chou et le choucroute*. When they encountered cabbage in the course of their westward incursions, they quickly adapted it to their requirements as a pickled vegetable, and later returned to market their invention both east and west.

Since the Middle Ages or earlier, sauerkraut was consumed in abundance between the Vosges and the Rhine. People ate it, but it did not constitute a dish on its own; it just accompanied whatever else was handy. The Alsatian chef Bommard presides over the luxurious restaurant « Kammerzell » resplendent with carved wood and a cast iron sign, standing across from the cathedral in Strasbourg. When he claims to have « invented » *choucroute aux poissons*, the older locals shrug their shoulders; as long as there have been pike and salmon swimming in the Rhine, fish has accompanied sauerkraut. Bommard just gets credit for reinventing the dish, in defiance of the quibbles of his colleagues, and that counts for something.

On the trail of *choucroute*

Choucroute is a straightforward, even prosaic dish, so inconsequential that Hansi, who is known as the herald of Alsatian identity, rarely shows *choucroute* in his pictures. There are just a few sketches for signs and a menu showing a couple sitting down at a table in front of a platter of cabbage garnished with sausages. Nevertheless, you will find *choucroute* everywhere. In the streets of Strasbourg and Colmar, it is on display like a culinary postcard. After traveling to Bangkok, Phillippe Schadt had the idea of giving new resonance to the dish by creating a « trail of choucroute » in Blaesheim, with about thirty « stops » to explore the variations on the theme. Only at his restaurant can you sample a *quiche à la choucroute*, a *choucroute au haddock*, and even a Vietnamese-style pasta with *choucroute* on special occasions.

Sausages ennobled

In the face of all these innovations, « traditional » *choucroute* still adheres pretty strictly to a set of rules. Flavored with juniper and thyme, the cabbage is simmered in a blend of goose fat and lard; apples, ham, sausage from Lorraine and sometimes *morteau* are added. Then come the Strasbourg sausages The cook might add *boudin noir* or liver dumplings, depending on his mood.

Choucroute alsacienne is not just a more or less calorific vegetable; it is also a complete main course fully capable of relating the history of Alsatian sausage making. « Alsatian *choucroute*, as it is known today,

Above
Monsieur Pfleger is one of the last growers who still harvests his cabbages by hand.

Facing page
A field of cabbages near Krautergersheim (which means « Cabbageville » in the Alsatian dialect) near Strasbourg.

> « At Yvonne in Strasbourg, members of the European parliament sit around a platter of choucroute *to talk things over between sessions.* »

originated at the end of the last century, » Oberlé explains. « It really received its patent of nobility in Paris, right after the War of 1870. » From 1860 on, the *charcutiers* of Alsace certainly lost no opportunity to display their products at expositions.

They shipped entire trains full of Alsatian beer, accompanied by the requisite *choucroute*. But when Alsace fell under German control, all bets were off. Many Alsatians made their way to Paris to set up establishments that appealed to high society, while the *charcutiers* and *choucroutiers* in exile set up their processing plants on the city's periphery. *Choucroute* became all the rage. Brillat-Savarin shared the excite-

ment and ranked the dish alongside *foie gras;* among the « gastronomic litmus tests of gentleman.».

Once the rules of the game were established, people began to bend them. Some chose to innovate, like Émile Jung in his three star restaurant Le Crocodile in Strasbourg, with his melange of sauerkraut and green cabbage seasoned with coriander and accompanied by frogs' legs. Others adhere to tradition. With a huge marquee, charming dovecotes, and geraniums in every windowbox, Krautergersheim celebrates sauerkraut as a capital city should. It's an obligatory calling for a community, whose very name means « cabbage city » in the Alsatian dialect.

Émile Jung's *cuisses de grenouilles poêlées et mille choux à la coriandre*

Émile Jung, the Michelin three-star chef of the restaurant Le Crocodile in Strasbourg, reinvents *choucroute* in this dish. He incorporates fresh cabbage and frogs' legs, both important products of the Alsatian countryside.

Serves 6
Preparation time : 45 minutes
Cooking time : 1 hour

1 lb., 12 oz. frogs' legs
4 1/4 oz. green cabbage cut in 1-inch wide slivers
6 cabbage leaves, cut in half
14 oz. cooked sauerkraut
3 sprigs of fresh cilantro
1 shallot
1 ounce butter
17 oz. veal stock (You may also use freeze dried veal stock.)
6 tablespoons of Madeira
salt and pepper

1- Peel and chop the shallot and cook briefly over high heat, stirring. Add the frogs' legs and let them brown. Add the Madeira and then the veal stock. Cook the frogs' legs over low heat for 30 minutes, basting them regularly. When they are done, drain them and set aside. Reduce the cooking sauce by half.
2- Immerse the halved cabbage leaves in salted water for 2 minutes. Pat them dry and place them on a sheet of greaseproof paper and let them dry out in a pre-heated 140° oven for 6 minutes. Salt and pepper them and keep them warm.
3- Cook the cabbage slivers in boiling salted water for 10 minutes. Add 3 pinches of chopped coriander leaves to the sauerkraut and re-heat gently in a pot, or for 3 minutes in a microwave oven.
4- Glaze the frogs' legs by basting them several times with the Madeira sauce.
5- Mound the sauerkraut in the center of 6 plates. Surround it with the cabbage slivers. Arrange the frogs' legs decoratively on top of the sauerkraut. Place a leaf of the dried cabbage on each plate. Pour the rest of the Madeira sauce around the frogs' legs and serve.

La choucroute de poisson

There are many variations on *choucroute*, but this is a « genuine » modern recipe based on tradition. It has become an instant classic!

Serves 6
Preparation time : 30 minutes
Resting time : 15 minutes
Cooking time : 55 minutes

2 lbs, 3 oz. raw sauerkraut
14 oz. salmon filet
14 oz. cod filet
10 1/2 oz. sole filet
10 1/2 oz. haddock
20 oz. Riesling
6 3/4 oz. white wine vinegar
5 1/4 oz. butter
6 3/4 oz. *crème fraîche*
3 shallots
8 juniper berries
8 peppercorns
Coarse salt, freshly ground pepper

1- Place the sauerkraut in a pot with 17 oz. of the Riesling, the juniper berries and the peppercorns. Add coarse salt to taste and cook 40 minutes over low heat. All the liquid should be absorbed.
2- Season the fish pieces with salt and pepper and let them rest 15 minutes on a platter.
3- Prepare the *beurre blanc*. Peel the shallots and mince them finely. Put them in a pot with the remaining wine and the vinegar over a very low heat, just until the liquid has evaporated. Place the pot over a double boiler. Add the butter cut into small pieces one at a time, whisking constantly. Add the *crème fraîche* and continue to « inflate » the *beurre blanc*, whisking gently. Add salt and pepper to taste.
4- 10 minutes before serving, cook the fish in a steamer for 5 minutes.
5- Place the sauerkraut on a warm porcelain platter. Arrange the fish decoratively on top and coat lightly with the *beurre blanc*. Serve the remaining sauce separately with the steamed potatoes.

La choucroute de chou rouge et pigeon à la chinoise

This easily prepared dish pays homage to the Asian origins of sauerkraut.

1- Wash the red cabbage and grate it in a food processor. Peel and core the apples and cut them into small cubes.

2- Melt the goose fat in a large pot and add the grated cabbage, the red wine, the raisins, the diced apple, the coriander seeds, and the *bouquet garni*. Season with salt and pepper. Cook over low heat for 40 minutes, stirring frequently.

3- Peel and chop the garlic. Season the pigeons with salt and pepper and cut them in half lengthwise.

4- Heat the oil in a frying pan. Cook the pigeons briefly over high heat; when they are lightly browned, add the honey and chopped garlic. Let the honey caramelize, then add the vinegar and soy sauce. Cook the pigeons 50 minutes, basting them very frequently with the cooking juices.

5- Combine the pigeons, sauce and red cabbage. Let the mixture simmer 30 minutes. Correct the seasonings and serve.

Serves 6
Preparation time : 35 minutes
Cooking time : 2 hours 10 minutes

6 small farm raised pigeons, ready to cook
1 red cabbage, weighing about 2 lbs.
4 garlic cloves
2 Golden Delicious apples
3 1/2 oz. raisins
17 oz. red wine
3 oz. balsamic vinegar
3/4 ounce honey
10 oz. soy sauce
1 3/4 oz. goose fat
3 tablespoons peanut oil
10 dry coriander seeds
1 *bouquet garni*
salt and pepper

The North

Le waterzooï de poulet

Serves 6
Preparation time : 35 minutes
Cooking time : 50 minutes

1 farm raised chicken, cut into 6 pieces
2 large onions
4 sprigs of parsley
6 carrots
2 leeks
1 stalk of celery
1 *bouquet garni*
3 1/2 oz. butter
17 oz. chicken stock (You may also use freeze dried chicken stock.)
4 egg yolks
63/4 oz. cream
salt and pepper

1- Wash the onions, carrots, leeks, and celery and cut them into fairly wide julienne strips. Melt the butter in a pot and add the vegetables. Cook 5 minutes, without allowing them to brown.
2- Add the chicken pieces, the parsley, and the bouquet garni. Add salt and pepper, pour over the chicken stock and cook covered over low heat for 45 minutes, stirring occasionally.
3- Mix the egg yolks and the cream in a large bowl. When the chicken pieces are cooked, drain them and place on a serving platter.
4- Remove the chicken's cooking liquid from the heat and add the yolk and cream mixture gradually, stirring to blend. Correct the sauce's seasoning and nap the chicken pieces with the sauce. Serve the *waterzooï* with slices of buttered toast.

Le coq à la bière

Serves 6
Preparation time : 20 minutes
Cooking time : 2 hours 40 minutes

3 lbs., 5 oz. rooster or chicken, cut into serving pieces
10 1/2 oz. smoked bacon
3 oz. chicken liver
2 slices of raw ham
1 quart Alsatian beer
1 onion
1 *bouquet garni*
1 1/4 oz. oil
1 3/4 oz. flour
6 slices of bread
salt and pepper

1- Peel and chop the onion. Cut the bacon into small pieces. Heat the oil in a pan and cook the rooster pieces over high heat for 10 minutes, letting them brown lightly.
2- Add the onion, the bacon, the *bouquet garni*, and the flour.
Turn the rooster pieces to coat them with the flour and pour the beer over all. Season with salt and pepper and cook over low heat 2 1/2 hours.
3- Chop the chicken livers and the ham slices. 20 minutes before the rooster has finished cooking, add the liver and ham to the pot and stir to combine.
4- Toast the bread slices and arrange them on a large serving platter. Place the rooster pieces on the bread, correct the seasoning and cover the rooster and bread with the cooking sauce. Serve very hot with steamed or fried potatoes.

La tarte au sucre

Serves 6
Preparation time : 10 minutes
Resting time : 3 hours 10 minutes
Cooking time : 20 minutes

For the pastry
8 3/4 oz. flour
1 egg
4 3/4 oz. butter, softened
3 1/2 oz. milk
1/2 oz. baker's yeast
1/3 oz. granulated sugar
pinch of salt

For the topping
2 eggs
2 tablespoons of liquid *crème fraîche*
2 3/4 oz. light brown sugar

1- Prepare the tart shell. Mix the yeast and sugar with the milk and let the mixture stand 10 minutes.
2- Put the flour in a shallow bowl and make a well in the center. Add the egg, the butter cut up into small pieces, the salt, and the yeast, sugar and milk mixture. Combine the ingredients with your fingertips and form the dough into a ball. Let it rest in a warm place for 1 hour.
3- Roll out the dough with a rolling pin and let it rise in a tart pan for about 2 hours in a warm place.
4- Preheat the oven to 410°. Prepare the topping. Beat the eggs and cream together vigorously. Spread the mixture over the dough, to within 1-inch of the rim. Sprinkle with the brown sugar and bake for 20 minutes.
5- Remove the tart to a plate and serve while still quite warm.

Lorraine

La quiche lorraine

Serves 6
Preparation time : 20 minutes
Resting time : 1 hour 10 minutes
Cooking time : 40 minutes

For the pastry
8 3/4 oz. flour
1 egg yolk
4 1/2 oz. butter, softened
pinch of salt

For the topping
4 1/2 oz. smoked bacon
2 3/4 oz. grated cheese (optional)
1 3/4 oz. *crème fraîche*
4 eggs
salt and pepper

1- Prepare the pastry shell. Put the flour in a large bowl and add the butter, cut up into small pieces, the salt, and the egg yolk. Mix together with your fingertips, adding enough water (about 2 oz.) to make the dough smooth. Wrap the dough in a towel and place it in the refrigerator for 1 hour.
2- Press the dough into a tart pan and prick the bottom with a fork. Return it to the refrigerator for 10 minutes to rest.
3- Preheat the oven to 350°. Prepare the topping. Cut the bacon into small pieces. Beat the eggs and cream together in a bowl as if making an omelet. Season with salt and pepper.
4- Remove the tart shell from the refrigerator, scatter the bacon pieces and grated cheese on top, and pour over the cream and egg mixture. Bake 40 minutes.
5- When the top is well browned, remove the quiche from the oven and let it rest 15 minutes before serving.

Alsace

Le kouglof

Serves 6
Preparation time : 30 minutes
Resting time : 2 hours
Cooking time : 1 hour

1lb. 1 oz. flour
7 3/4 oz. butter, softened and cut up into small pieces, plus 1 3/4 oz. for the cake mold
1 1/2 oz. granulated sugar
3 eggs
3 1/2 oz. *crème fraîche*
5 ounces lukewarm milk
1/2 ounce brewer's yeast
2 tablespoons Kirsch
5 1/4 oz. raisins
1 3/4 oz. slivered almonds
3/4 oz. confectioners' sugar
pinch of salt

1- Combine the flour, the butter, the sugar, the salt, and the eggs in a bowl and mix them together with your fingertips. Add the yeast dissolved in the warm milk, the Kirsch, and the raisins. Add the *crème fraîche* and work the dough gently until it just comes away easily from your hand.
2- Butter a *kouglof* mold, sprinkle the almonds over the bottom, and fill half-way up with the dough.
3- Cover the mold with a damp towel and let it rest about 2 hours in a warm place. Preheat the oven to 340°.
4- When the dough has risen thoroughly, bake the *kouglof* 1 hour.

Remove it from the mold and sprinkle with the confectioners' sugar before serving.

Le baekenofe

Serves 6
Preparation time : 30 minutes
Marinating time : overnight
Cooking time : 2 hours 30 minutes

10 1/2 oz. mutton shoulder
10 1/2 oz. pork shoulder
10 1/2 oz. beef chuck
1 cooked pig's trotter
2 lbs. potatoes
4 large onions
4 garlic cloves
1 *bouquet garni*
1 bottle of Alsatian white wine
1 3/4 oz. butter to grease the terrine
salt and pepper

1- The night before you prepare the *baekenofe*, peel and chop 2 of the onions and crush the garlic cloves. In a deep bowl, place the meat, cut up into pieces, the *bouquet garni*, the chopped onions, the garlic cloves, and half of the white wine. Let these ingredients marinate overnight.
2- The next day, peel and cut up the potatoes and the two other onions. Butter a large earthenware terrine and cover the bottom with a layer of about 2/3 of the potatoes and the onions.
3- Add the marinated meats, the garlic cloves, and the *bouquet garni*. Strain the marinade and pour it over the terrine together with the rest of the white wine. Season with salt and pepper.
4- Sprinkle the remaining onions over the top and finish with a layer of the remaining potato slices.
5- Cover the terrine and bake it at 320° for 2 1/2 hours without uncovering it. When you are ready to serve, bring the terrine to the dining table. Remove the cover in front of your guests so they can enjoy the mouthwatering fragrance of the *baekenofe*.

Le flammenküche

Serves 6
Preparation time : 20 minutes
Cooking time : 35 minutes

21 oz. bread dough
8 3/4 oz. *thick crème fraîche*
2 1/2 oz. butter
8 3/4 oz. smoked bacon
3 large onions
3/4 ounce rapeseed oil
salt and pepper

1- Peel and mince the onions. Melt the butter in a frying pan and cook the minced onions in the butter, stirring, for 20 minutes, without letting them take on color, until they are very soft.
2- Cut the bacon into strips and sauté it in a pan without added fat. Preheat the oven to its highest setting.
3- Roll out 6 equal portions of the bread dough into rectangles 2-inches thick. Spread equal amounts of the *crème fraîche*, the «melted» onions, and the bacon on top of each rectangle. Season with salt and pepper. Bake 10 minutes.
4- When the *flammenküche* are golden and crusty, remove them from the oven. Sprinkle them with a little rapeseed oil and serve immediately with a glass of good beer.

The Ardennes

Les pieds de porc Sainte-Menehould

Serves 6
Preparation time : 30 minutes
Salting time : 3 hours
Cooking time: 4 hours 30 minutes

6 pig's trotters (well cleaned by your butcher)
1 onion
2 carrots
2 shallots
2 garlic cloves, crushed
1 *bouquet garni*
2 cloves
1 large glass of white wine
8 3/4 oz. soft white bread crumbs
2 eggs
3 1/2 oz. butter
17 3/4 oz. coarse salt
salt and pepper

1- Cover the pig's trotters in the coarse salt for 3 hours. Peel the carrots, shallots, and onion. Tie up each trotter with strips of cloth cut from an old towel to prevent them from disintegrating while they cook.
2- Put the following ingredients into a pot and cover with water: the onion, carrots, garlic, shallots, *bouquet garni*, trotters, white wine, and cloves. Season with salt and pepper and simmer 4 hours over low heat.
3- When the meat on the trotters is very tender, drain them, and set aside to cool. Remove the cloth strips and cut the trotters lengthwise.
4- Melt the butter. Break the eggs and beat them as you would for an omelet. Dip the trotters in the beaten egg, then in the soft bread crumbs, and cook them for 30 minutes on the barbecue grill or under the oven broiler, sprinkling them with the melted butter.
Serve very hot with mustard and a puree of split peas.
Instead of grilling the breaded trotters, you may also cook them in a pan, letting them brown in melted butter. Veal heads and feet may be prepared in the same way.

the center

Boeuf bourguignon from the Charolais region

Charolais cattle, bred in the shadow of the abbey of Cluny, represent the very finest in French beef. Their homeland is a countryside of pastures bordered by hedgerows, woodlands and livestock fairs. A few vines may manage to take hold in some hidden patches of land. There is no Burgundian cuisine without wine, after all.

Above
A very old stone wall surrounds the market hall in Saint-Christophe-en-Brionnais. This is the spot where payment is made, usually in cash, for bargains struck at the weekly cattle market.

Facing page
With their cream colored coats, thick necks and docile natures, Charolais cattle have been carefully bred for almost two hundred years. Their well-marbled meat is as succulent as anyone could desire, and can be found on tables all over France. This beef is the basis of boeuf bourguignon.

Jean-Noël Dauvergne's restaurant on the Place de Poisson near Charolles is booked solid every Sunday year round. People come for his *duo de charolais*, a rather off-beat local specialty. A perfectly cooked portion of rumpsteak and a little helping of *boeuf bourguinon* are presented side by side on the same plate. Sometimes oxtails cooked in red wine are substituted for the *boeuf bourguignon*, but the underlying concept remains the same: the goal is to demonstrate the nobility of the beef, not only by offering its most costly cuts, but also by showing how to prepare the more proletarian portions. Jean-Noël was born amidst these pastures, gentle hills, and little valleys between the Charolais and Brionnais regions, where the spirit of the great abbey of Cluny once held sway. He grew up steeped in the quasi-religion of the local cattle that are named for the region. He has now set up shop between the town of Charolles and Saint-Christophe-en-Brionnais, a village whose cattle market has just celebrated five hundred years of great

feasts and good bargains. Jean-Noël still recalls the aroma of beef stew simmering all morning long on his grandmother's woodburning stove. Day after day, he pays faithful homage to this simple yet sophisticated dish. It is a family meal, almost a private memory.

A family meal
Restaurants catering to tourists in Burgundy rarely list *boeuf bourguignon* on their menus. These days, the trend is away from substantial sauces. But Burgundy is the place where this dish, now prepared all over France, originated; you will still find it served as the *plat du jour* in small village cafes or roadhouses where the local postman might stop for a midday meal.

> « It's an inexpensive meal, easy to reheat when there's a big crowd, and, most importantly, it's a dish that's really our own. »

The dish might be served on Sundays when families get together in the kitchens of stone farmhouses, or set out on long tables for village festivals. « There's a *bourguignon* that's sacred here, » says Pierre Grillet, a cattle breeder in Vitry near Paray-le-Monial. « It gets all the neighbors together on the second Saturday in September. » He remembers coming home from the fair where he had sold a cow after haggling with a butcher, who did not necessarily work with an offi-

Le boeuf bourguignon

The secret of a fine *boeuf bourguignon* is simmering the meat for hours over a very low heat.

Serves 6
Preparation time : 30 minutes
Cooking time : 3 hours

2 lbs., 3 oz. stewing beef cut into large cubes
2 quarts red wine
17 oz. *fond de veau* (You may also use freeze dried veal stock.)
10 1/2 oz. small onions
10 1/2 oz. bacon
8 3/4 oz. cultivated mushrooms
4 garlic cloves, crushed with skins on
1 3/4 oz. flour
1 3/4 oz. butter
5 oz. peanut oil
1 *bouquet garni*
1 ounce granulated sugar
salt and pepper

1- Heat 3 1/2 oz. of the peanut oil in a pot. Brown the beef cubes on all sides. Lower the heat, and add the *bouquet garni* and the garlic cloves. Simmer a few minutes, then stir in the flour.

2- Pour in the red wine and the *fond de veau*. Season with salt and pepper. Skim, then lower the heat and simmer for 3 hours, stirring occasionally.

3- Peel the onions and caramelize them in a pot with the butter, the sugar and 1/2 cup of water. Keep warm.

4- Rinse the mushrooms and cut them in half. Sauté them with the bacon and the remaining oil. Let them brown for 5 minutes, then add them to the onions.

5- When the stew meat is cooked and very tender, place the pieces on a serving platter. Add the onions, mushrooms, and bacon with their juices to the cooking liquid.

6- Simmer a few minutes longer. Correct the seasonings and cover the meat with the sauce. Serve very hot with pasta or steamed potatoes.

Above left
Smocks and berets at the cattle market in Saint-Christophe-en-Brionnais. This event brings together all of the region's breeders, feeders, and wholesalers.

Above right
Door of a cattle truck on market day.

Facing page left
Henri Velut, a cattle feeder and breeder in the Brionnais region.

Facing page right
Cows have increasingly replaced steers, which used to be used for working in the fields.

cially certified abattoir in those days. « Once we agreed on a price and bargained back and forth a while, I'd ask the butcher for some stew meat or some other cut good for making a *pot-au-feu*. Generally, he'd give it to me; it didn't cost him much. »

An unassuming, crowd-pleasing peasant meal, *boeuf bourguignon* is a dish fit for connoisseurs who do not need to flaunt their knowledge. It is the antithesis of roast beef, for example, and is considered the poor relation of a *daube*. Even the red wine so generously poured into a *bourguignon* fails to give it aristocratic airs. Only a purist like Jean-Noël Dauvergne would insist on using a fine Givry or Rully in his recipe. A very simple wine will do the job, as long as it is rustic and full-bodied, like the unpretentious blends that used to be made on every farm to brighten bleak winter days. This is a region where you will still see little patches of vines that seem almost secretive, as if they were pilfering a bit of pastureland. Farther east in the area of Bresse, isolated rows of vines are planted on the slopes to mark boundaries between parcels of land; they used to suffice to fill a household's wine barrels for the year.

The ultimate in French beef

Burgundians had no difficulty in making their little Sunday treat into a national dish, a classic in all the manuals of French cuisine. Their skill at winemaking and their reputation for cattle breeding were sufficient to gain the necessary entrees. The Charolais breed actually originated in Oyé, in the Brionnais region, some forty kilometers from Charolles. Here you will find a handful of houses, a town hall, a cafe-restaurant where a *bourguignon* is offered as a treat for the old timers, and a sign that says it all: this is indeed the « cradle of the breed.» Brionnais, Charolais: the different nuances escape the visitor who is just passing through; they see

> « *There aren't many restaurants that offer boeuf bourguignon on their menus; it's a dish that's cooked at home.* »

meadows and hedges that look very much alike. But in the eyes of professionals, the slight differences are worth their weight in gold. Brionnais grass is apparently even better, richer, more distinctive. The story goes back to the eighteenth century, when two breeders became aware of a phenomenon not yet called « market development.» They noted increasing urbanization and a growing prosperous middle class who enjoyed eating meat; there was a demand here that butchering dairy cows at the end of their useful lives could not really satisfy. They saw the opportunity to raise animals for meat, breeding them with that goal in mind.

The two breeders began in Lyon, the closest big city, and then looked farther afield. They walked all the way to Paris—a seventeen-day journey—driving a herd of almost a thousand head of cattle. Most importantly, they established the standards for a new breed. A Charolais was an animal raised exclusively for its meat, one huge muscle as juicy and well-marbled as anyone could desire. Agricultural shows and competitions accomplished the rest over the next two centuries; the cattle got heavier and heavier, more

and more magnificent. Charolais, sporting red, white and blue ribbons at every *Salon de l'agriculture*, are recognized as the ultimate in French beef.

Cattle markets, a French institution

These developments were great news for the dealers, butchers, *emboucheurs* (who fatten cattle rather than breeding them) and other wholesalers and middlemen who have frequented Saint-Christophe-en-Brionnais since the Middle Ages. This curious town dozes for six days out of seven, until once a week it is jolted awake by the influx of crowds and feverish activity. The covered market at the end of the main street has grown more and more enormous, gradually assuming the dimensions and the architecture of a vast railway terminus.

Every Thursday morning, men in smocks and berets circulate, appraising and sizing up these white-coated animals with an experienced eye. The cattle are dis-

played in various categories: cows, heifers, and, best of all in these suspicious times, « certified animals.» Not long ago, the bargain was sealed in cash; now it is settled by check, a little to one side of the fray by a famous enclosure known as the *Mur d'argent* (« Wall of Money »). Then the counterparties head off to celebrate in one of four neighborhood restaurants. What is the first choice of these market professionals? *Tête de veau* or *pot-au-feu* « because it gives a man strength, » claims the owner of the Restaurant du Midi, a bar cum cafe-newsstand, and headquarters for the local soccer club association.

Beef simmered lovingly with little onions, thyme, and wine—a *bourguignon* is for other times, more ordinary occasions. Often it's a dish enjoyed by diners who don't give a thought to the Charolais cattle who flourish in Burgundian pastures.

Le coq au vin

In Burgundian farmhouses, roosters, which also require long slow cooking, are prepared « au vin » like certain cuts of beef.

Serves 6 to 8
Preparation time : 40 minutes
Cooking time : 3 hours

1 rooster cut up into large pieces
1 large onion
8 3/4 oz. pearl onions
2 garlic cloves, crushed with skin on
10 1/2 oz. bacon
10 1/2 oz. cultivated mushrooms
2 quarts red Burgundy wine
1 3/4 oz. oil
4 1/2 oz. butter
1 tablespoon flour
1 *bouquet garni*
3 sprigs of Italian parsley
1/2 ounce teaspoon granulated sugar
salt and pepper

1- Heat the oil in a cast iron pot. Brown the rooster pieces on all sides. Add the large onion, coarsely chopped, the garlic cloves and the *bouquet garni*. Lower the heat and cook 5 minutes. Stir in the flour.

2- Pour over the red wine. Season with salt and pepper. Simmer the rooster for 3 hours over low heat.

3- 1 hour before serving, peel the pearl onions. Heat 1 3/4 oz. of the butter in a pot. Cook the pearl onions briefly over high heat in the foaming butter. Add the sugar and the bacon and cook together several minutes.

4- Wash the mushrooms and cut them in half. Add them to the onion-bacon mixture and cook together for another 10 minutes.

5- When you are ready to serve, place the rooster pieces on a serving platter. Put the onion-bacon-mushroom mixture and its cooking juices into the wine sauce and return to a boil. Whisk in the rest of the butter.

Correct the seasonings and cover the pieces of rooster with the sauce. Garnish with the parsley sprigs and serve very hot with steamed potatoes or pasta.

Le bourguignon de légumes aux herbes potagères

Traditional recipes « à la bourguignon » involve cooking with red wine. You can easily prepare vegetables using the same method.

Serves 6
Preparation time : 40 minutes
Cooking time : 55 minutes

1 quart of red wine
10 1/2 oz. bacon
6 3/4 oz. *fond de veau* (You may also use freeze dried veal stock.)
1 large onion
3 garlic cloves
14 oz. carrots
1 leek
10 1/2 oz. cultivated mushrooms
8 3/4 oz. fava beans
2 Golden Delicious apples
1 3/4 oz. butter
1 bunch of tarragon
1 *bouquet garni*
3 sprigs of parsley
salt and pepper

1- Peel and mince the garlic and onion. Peel and quarter the apples. Cut the carrots into rounds. Clean the mushrooms. Wash the leek and slice it into 10 pieces. Cook the beans in a pot of boiling water for 1 minute and remove them from their skins. Wash and coarsely chop the tarragon and parsley.

2- Melt the butter in a large, heavy bottomed pot. Brown the onion, garlic, and bacon in the warm butter, then add the mushrooms, carrots, leek, and *bouquet garni*. Add salt and pepper and pour over the red wine. Reduce by half over low heat.

3- Add the *fond de veau* and simmer the vegetables gently for 40 minutes. Add the quartered apples and beans and cook 10 minutes more over low heat.

4- Correct the seasonings. Add the fresh herbs and steep them with the sauce and warm vegetables for 5 minutes. Serve immediately.

Estofinado in Aveyron

Spoken with the right accent, the word for « stockfish » becomes « *estofi* ». In Aveyron it is prepared as a kind of *brandade* with a base of unsalted dried cod. This recipe is as old as the River Lot, which links this inland region with the Atlantic, but it was rediscovered in the nineteenth century by the miners of Decazeville.

Above
The stockfish that used to be towed up the Lot from Bordeaux was so hard and dry that it could only be cut with a saw.

Facing page
The Druilhes sisters prepare estofinado in the kitchen of their inn on the banks of the Lot in the early days of autumn. People come from all over the region to savor this ancestral dish, which no one has the time to cook at home any more.

When Pierrot remembers those Sunday family gatherings where they feasted like lords, he speaks with a tremor in his voice. Thirty-two years working in the mines, forty years of retirement–his memories go back to the era when Decazeville was the prosperous capital of the « Pays Noir » . It had a railway station and its shops did a brisk business. There were slag heaps at the end of streets, smokestacks in the distance and weeks of sweating in the mines. Come Sunday, no one was pinching pennies. « We were pretty well paid. We'd head up to the plateau at Almon-les-Junies and treat ourselves to stuffed chicken and sausages. Then came *estofinado*. Just seeing it made you hungry all over again. » Almon-les-Junies was the weekend country retreat for laborers from the mineshafts.
« La Decouverte », the last active mine in the area, will soon close, and the zinc factory in Vivez isn't what it once was. On the hillsides, pine trees hide the scars left by the mining machinery a little more each day. But every

autumn when the new wine is ready, Pierrot takes the bus back to Almon. Nothing has changed up there. The three cafes he remembers from his youth are still open. They have even begun to prosper again since people started coming from all over the Southwest to eat this strange *brandade* with eggs and walnut oil, prepared with stockfish, not dried salt cod. Spoken with the local accent, stockfish becomes « *estofi* », whence the name « *estofinado* », a dish that the miners learned to enjoy just as much as the farmers did.

> « The old timers remember how they used to soak the stockfish right in the streams or village fountains. »

**The codfish that went astray
on the Rouergue plateau**
For the thirty years he has been mayor of Almon-les-Junies, Gabriel Romiguière has taken his job seriously. Last year he undertook a journey to the source of his village's local specialty, all the way to the remote Lofoten islands in Norway. Upon his return, he decorated the rotary at the entrance to his village with a small codfish drier like the ones they use there, and he has posted signs all over the place proclaiming, « Almon-les-Junies, *Estofinado* Capital ». He is an absolute authority on the subject. « Whatever you

L'estofinado

You have to allow time to prepare *estofinado*. The stockfish has to be soaked before cooking. Old-timers remember immersing it in streams or village fountains.

Serves 6
Preparation time : 45 minutes
Soaking time : 24 hours
Cooking time : 2 hours 45 minutes

1 lb. stockfish (dried unsalted cod)
5 eggs
3 1/2 oz. thick *crème fraîche* (optional)
1 lb., 12 oz. small firm potatoes
1 bunch of parsley
1 onion
6 garlic cloves
2 bay leaves
1 *bouquet garni*
3 1/2 oz. walnut oil
salt and freshly ground pepper

1- The day before you prepare the *estofinado*, put the stockfish in a large container of cold water, and soak it for 24 hours. Change the water frequently.
2- When you are ready to prepare the dish, cut up the stockfish into large pieces and peel and chop the onion.
3- Combine the stockfish, 3 garlic cloves, the onion, the bay leaves, and the *bouquet garni* in a large pot. Pour over 1 quart of cold water and simmer over low heat for about 2 hours. Let the fish cool in its cooking liquid, then drain it and flake it with a fork, removing any small bones.
4- Cook the potatoes in boiling salted water for 30 minutes. Peel them and mash them coarsely with a fork.
5- Cook the eggs for 10 minutes in boiling water, run them under cold water, and shell and chop them.
6- Wash and chop the parsley. Peel and chop the remaining garlic cloves. Combine the fish, the potatoes, the eggs, the garlic and the parsley in a pot. Correct the seasonings.
7- Heat the walnut oil in a skillet. When it is almost bubbling, pour it over the stockfish. Cook the mixture over high heat for 2 minutes. Add the *crème fraîche* at the last moment and serve very hot.

Gabriel Romiguière, the mayor of Almon-les-Junies, is proud that his village is the world capital of estofinado. He took an educational trip to the Lofoten islands and returned with a Norwegian codfish dryer that now stands at the crossroads at the entry to Almon.

do, don't say to soak your stockfish to remove the salt, » he explains.

That technique is reserved for traditional salt cod. Both start with the same fish, cod or haddock, but they are preserved differently. Stockfish is simply dried, not salted. It may seem surprising that the emblematic dish of the southwestern reaches of the Massif Central, from Aveyron in the north all the way to Châtaigneraie in Cantal, should be *estofinado*. This is a recipe based upon a fish dried stiff as a board that has to be cut with a saw before being soaked overnight. When you consider the River Lot, which links the interior to the Atlantic, flowing through the rugged countryside with twists and turns, you would be more likely to expect fried river fish and trout with bacon as the specialty.

There are numerous theories about how stockfish was introduced into Aveyron. Some say it was a gift from the Vikings, dating back to their passage through the Auvergne, or a legacy of the pilgrims on the road to Campostella. Perhaps it was a trophy brought back by Aveyron soldiers from their military campaigns in Holland, or an invention of veterans of Napoleon's army. The very abundance of hypotheses is proof in itself of the deep roots of a dish whose reality is inextricably mingled with its legend. There is only one tangible record to be found, a complaint lodged with Montaubon's commercial court in 1780 by a merchant from Villefranche-de-Rouergue against one of his colleagues relating to non-payment for a delivery of « stofic.»

Mysteries of stockfish

It seems most likely that stockfish arrived via the Lot. Although only a few canoes venture on the river these days, it was navigable and navigated until 1926.

A small boat on the Lot, a reminder of the times when the gabariers, those mariners who navigated the river all the way to Bordeaux, returned to teach the residents of the interior about a fish that came from the other side of the ocean.

Colbert installed a system of locks and the towpaths were well maintained; the railroad was slow to make competitive inroads.

The Lot was the only way to reach the ocean. The river teemed with *gabariers*, ferrymen who took oak from the Auvergne, cheeses from Aubrac, and coal from Aubin and Cransac to Bordeaux. On the return trip, they brought back wine, a smattering of dry goods and hardware, and stockfish, all purchased in the port of Bordeaux. The *gabariers* used the stockfish for bartering and, to make the product more appealing, they towed it behind their boats to soften it. Since it took about ten days along the towpath to reach their destination, the stockfish arrived in an edible state.

Marie-Rose has been preparing *estofinado* for about thirty years. She runs a little inn at the end of the old bridge over the Livinhac, not far from Decazeville. « You have to select good potatoes and cook them just right. You flake the cod with two forks. Keep the dishes warm in a *bain-marie*. You absolutely must have the right place to soak the fish; otherwise, watch out for the smell. »

Modest but proud, the image of its homeland

Estofinado is usually prepared on Fridays in the Rouergue. On fast days, *estofinado* was naturally eaten in farmsteads as salt cod dishes were elsewhere. Since

« *It may look simple to prepare* estofinado, *but it really takes a lot of skill.* »

the Rouergue long remained a bastion of Catholicism in a largely Protestant region, the rules were rigorously observed.

In Almon-les-Junies, however, *estofinado* is reserved for Sundays, and this shift sums up the melding of two worlds, the rural and the urban, of peasants and laborers, in one dish. Since the Duke of Decazes founded this town 170 years ago, the two groups of people have gone hand in hand.

Although there were mines in the region, there were no mining villages. Men who became mineworkers continued to manage small family holdings, and maintained their ties to the peasants' rural world. Starting in the early 1800s, laborers immigrated en masse from Italy and Spain, countries where cod is relished both salted and dried. Despite its rustic origins, *estofinado* became a dish for people of modest means in the city, both locals and immigrant workers. It was natural for them to enjoy it on Sunday, their one day off.

World War II furthered this trend. « We were better off in the country than people were in towns, » the mayor of Almon goes on. « Miners came here to improve on their everyday fare and to do their shopping for the week. That's how they got into the habit of ordering our *estofinado*, which we'd usually eat when we were harvesting grapes, or serve on evenings when neighbors would come over to help us crack nuts before taking them to the mill. » Humble tillers of the soil sat elbow to elbow with the heroic laborers of the murky mine pits, and thus a very unassuming dish tells an important story.

L'estoficado

This is the most popular traditional meal of Nice. Although this recipe is brightened up with Mediterranean flavors, it is still a close cousin of *estofinado*.

Serves 6
Preparation time : 1 hour
Soaking time : 24 hours
Cooking time : 4 hours

2 lbs., 3 oz. stockfish (unsalted dried cod)
4 lbs., 6 oz. very ripe tomatoes
2 lbs., 3 oz. small new potatoes
4 large onions
4 peppers
5 garlic cloves
1 *bouquet garni*
1 bay leaf
10 1/2 oz. Niçoise olives
1 cup *marc* brandy
8 1/2 oz. olive oil
salt and pepper

1- The day before you prepare the *estoficado*, place the stockfish in a large container and cover it with cold water. Soak for 24 hours, changing the water frequently.

2- The day you prepare the dish, cut the stockfish flesh from the skin using a large knife. Set the skin and small bones aside. Put the cut-up fish in a container, wash it once more, and drain.

3- Combine the skin and bones in a stew pot with 2 of the onions, peeled and chopped, 1 crushed garlic clove, and the bay leaf. Simmer 1 hour over low heat. Strain the broth.

4- Heat the olive oil in a large pot with a heavy base. Sauté the pieces of fish several minutes, stirring with a wooden spatula. When the stockfish is a light gold, pour in the brandy and add the remaining onions, peeled and chopped, 4 garlic cloves, peeled and minced, the *bouquet garni*, the tomatoes, and the peppers cut into long slices. Add salt and a generous amount of pepper and simmer covered for at least 3 hours, adding broth from time to time to prevent the stockfish from drying out.

5- Add the olives and the potatoes, peeled and halved, to the pot. Cook 1 hour more over low heat.

Serve the *estoficado* in deep soup bowls with olive oil on the side. It is traditional to drizzle olive oil over each bowl.

La brandade de morue pommes vapeur

This recipe for « *brandade à la provençale* », which is prepared with salt cod, has many similarities to *estofinado*. The flavors of each dish are as delectable as they are different.

1- The day before you cook the dish, place the salt cod in a container and soak it for 24 hours, changing the water frequently.

2- On the day you prepare the *brandade*, peel the potatoes and steam them for 10 to 15 minutes.

3- Meanwhile, place the cod in a large pot, cover with cold water, add the *bouquet garni* and bring to a boil. Lower the heat and let the fish simmer 10 minutes. Drain the salt cod and put it on a large platter. Remove the skin and small bones and carefully flake the fish.

4- Heat 5 oz. of the olive oil in a pot and add the fish and minced garlic cloves. Simmer 5 minutes over low heat, stirring with a wooden spoon.

5- Remove from the heat. Gradually incorporate 8.5 oz. of the oil and the milk, stirring briskly (as you would for a mayonnaise). The *brandade* will gradually take on the consistency of a light puree. Add the lemon juice, salt, and a generous amount of pepper. Serve with the hot potatoes and slices of bread that have been brushed with olive oil and toasted 5 minutes in the oven.

You may use a food processor to emulsify the fish, milk, and oil. You may also mash the potatoes and add them to the cooking pot or food processor to combine them with the fish.

Serves 6
Preparation time : 25 minutes
Soaking time : 24 hours
Cooking time : 25 minutes

2 lbs., 3 oz. salt cod
2 lbs. potatoes
17 oz. olive oil at room temperature
8 1/2 oz. milk
2 garlic cloves, minced
a squeeze of lemon juice
1 *bouquet garni*
12 slices of country-style bread
salt and pepper

Le soufflé de morue aux pommes de terre à l'huile de noix

Aveyron is a walnut-growing region. This recipe marries the flavors of potatoes, fish and walnut oil, a combination that is the essence of this *soufflé*. The aromas and tastes blend, meld and rise together to produce a dish fit for a king. You may prepare the *soufflé* with traditional dried salt cod, or with stockfish; if using salt cod, you must soak the fish for 24 hours and use no more than 9 oz.

1- Cover the cod with cool water for 3 hours. Change the water each hour.

2- Cook the peeled potatoes in boiling water for 20 minutes. Drain them and mash them in a food mill with a little cooking water. Keep the puree warm.

3- Bring the milk to a boil with the bay leaf, the unpeeled garlic cloves and the nutmeg. Poach the cod in the warm milk mixture for 15 minutes. Remove the bay leaf and garlic cloves and mash the fish with a fork into the milk.

4- Pour the fish mixture over the potato puree, add the butter, cut in small pieces, and the walnut oil. Mix with a spatula until you have a smooth puree

5- Separate the egg whites from the yolks. Blend the yolks into the fish puree. Beat the egg whites to form firm peaks. Fold the whites carefully into the puree. Add salt and pepper.

6- Butter a *soufflé* mold and pour the mixture in. Cook in a slow oven at 340° for 30 to 35 minutes without opening the oven door. Serve immediately with a green salad.

Serves 6
Preparation time : 20 minutes
Soaking time : 3 hours
Cooking time : 1 hour 5 minutes

14 oz. fresh salted cod (pieces of cod filet salted with coarse salt)
6 medium firm-fleshed potatoes
6 3/4 oz. milk
2 3/4 oz. butter
3 eggs
3 tablespoons walnut oil
3 garlic cloves
1 bay leaf
pinch of grated nutmeg
salt and freshly ground pepper

Aligot and *truffade* in the Auvergne

Aligot in Aubrac, *truffade* in Cantal: these are sister dishes that evoke the highlands of the Auvergne where the grass is like green velvet. Potatoes and *tomme fraîche* are their basic ingredients. When that combination makes its way into a pot, the traditional culture of Auvergnat shepherds' huts comes back to life.

Above
The ancient practice of transhumance still marks the Rieucau's family life. Every spring, they depart at dawn to herd their cattle from Saint-Come-d'Olt in the valley to the highland pastures of Aubrac.

Facing page
Near the Reygade buron on the hillside of Puy Mary, cows are milked morning and evening and tomme is made every day. The cheeses are set out to drain on pieces of cloth, which are then washed and left to dry in the sun.

Every summer, Daniel, one of the last seven or eight migrating shepherds in Cantal, drives his herd up to graze in the high pastures. He spends five months housed in a *buron*, a small windowless building that stands alone on the far side of the mountain, flanked by a cheese press and molds. He gets up at first light and makes his cheese each morning and evening. The cylinders of cantal and salers are stacked like treasures in the ripening cave behind the hut. In the old days, men departed in groups, embarking for the countryside as sailors would for the sea. Today, Daniel climbs up the mountain in a four-wheel drive vehicle along with his wife and three children. The family spends the summer here with other ruined *burons* as their only neighbors. Few days pass without a visit from a group of hikers, who will buy a piece of cheese, and perhaps sit down to enjoy a *truffade*.

Truffade (the name comes from « *truf-fas* », the local dialect's word for « potato ») is the pride of the lofty Cantal highlands. Take a few potatoes, cut them up coarsely, put them in a skillet with a little pork fat and garlic, add cream, and at the last moment, a generous amount of two-day-old *tomme* to bind it all together. It is a dish dating back to the time when shepherds were not permitted to take a slice of aged cheese. They could use only *tomme fraîche* (milk that had been curdled and pressed, but still had to be broken up, salted, and put into molds before becoming what is considered cheese in these parts) to improve upon an ordinary dish of potatoes and bacon.

> « There's a long history on your fork when truffade *hangs down from it in ribbons.* »

A common ancestor
On the windy plateaus of Aubrac, a few dozen kilometers from Cantal, the enclosed grazing lands stretch as far as the eye can see. There are other ruined *burons* here, relics of a past that is fast disappearing. Here you will find the same trinity of ingredients: garlic, potatoes, and *tomme*. But in Aubrac, the potatoes are boiled and pureed, and this difference is enough to earn *truffade's* little sister a name of her own: *aligot*.

Aubrac lies on the pilgrimage route to Campostella, and this lends the dish a special significance. The

L'aligot

This is the happy marriage of *tomme fraîche* from Laguiole and pureed potatoes.

Serves 6
Preparation time : 30 minutes
Cooking time : 55 minutes

3 lbs., 5 oz. large potatoes
4 garlic cloves
5 1/2 oz. butter
8 3/4 oz. *crème fraîche*
18 oz. *tomme fraîche* from Laguiole
salt and freshly ground pepper

1- Peel the potatoes and cut them in large dice. Peel and mince the garlic cloves.
2- Cook the potatoes 35 minutes in boiling salted water. Drain them and put them through a food mill with the minced garlic.
3- Pour the puree into a large heavy-bottomed pot. Add the *crème fraîche*, the *tomme* cut up into small pieces, and the butter. Add salt and pepper and cook the mixture over low heat, stirring energetically for a long time with a wooden spatula, always in the same direction,
4- When the mixture no longer adheres to the sides of the pot and begins to form ribbons, the *aligot* is ready. Serve it, letting it stream down in ribbons from a spoon. Accompany the dish with Aubrac beef or grilled local sausages.

La truffade

In this recipe, *tomme* is combined with sautéed potatoes.

Serves 6
Preparation time : 35 minutes
Cooking time : 25 minutes

2 lbs. potatoes
2 garlic cloves, peeled and minced
7 oz. bacon
14 oz. *tomme fraîche* from Cantal
1 3/4 oz. butter
6 3/4 oz. *crème fraîche*
salt and freshly ground pepper

1- Melt the butter in a large skillet. Cook the bacon over high heat until it browns lightly.
2- Peel the potatoes and cut them into narrow strips. Add them to the bacon with the garlic. Add salt and pepper and let the mixture brown for 10 minutes.
3- Cut the *tomme* into small dice. Add the cheese and the *crème fraîche* to the potatoes. Cook 10 minutes, stirring carefully.
When the bottom of the *truffade* begins to brown, unmold it onto a platter and serve it very hot.

La galette d'aligot à la viande d'Aubrac marinée à la gentiane

You can easily make the leftover *aligot* into delicious *galettes* and serve them with *aubrac*, a local meat specialty.

Serves 6
Preparation time : 1 hour
Marinating time : 1 hour
Resting time : 20 minutes
Cooking time : 30 minutes

21 oz. leftover *aligot*
1 lb. 4 oz. top side of Aubrac beef
(You may use beef from another region.)
1 tablespoon of gentian liqueur
1 bunch of chives, washed and chopped
1 bunch of tarragon, washed and chopped
2 shallots, peeled and sliced
juice of 1 lime
4 tablespoons of olive oil
1 tablespoon of peanut oil
1 3/4 oz. butter
3 1/2 oz. flour
salt and freshly ground pepper

1- Cut the beef into very fine strips and then into small cubes. Marinate the meat with the gentian liqueur, the olive oil, the lime juice, the shallots, and the herbs on a platter in the refrigerator for 1 hour.
2- Drain the meat and mix it with the cold *aligot*. Add salt and pepper. Form the mixture into egg-sized balls with a spoon.
3- Lightly press down the balls of *aligot* to make thick pancakes. Coat them with flour and let them rest 20 minutes in the refrigerator.
4- Heat the butter and the peanut oil in a large skillet. Sauté the pancakes in sets of four in the foaming butter, browning them on both sides. Drain them and serve them hot and crusty with an endive salad dressed with walnut oil.

Above left
After being pressed, the cheese is cut up into curds, salted, and put into molds. Cheese from Salers then assumes its traditional shape.

Above right
In the old days, workers in the burons were not permitted to use any aged cheese. They would take what they needed from fresh tomme to make aligot and truffade. Ideally, the cheese would be two or three days old.

Facing page left
Tomme fraîche is difficult to find outside the Auvergne, but it is essential for making both aligot and truffade. During the 1960s, the cooperative Jeune Montagne distributed the cheese free to organizers of local festivals, inaugurating the tradition of giant aligots.

Facing page right
It is an absolute requirement that aligot and truffade spin into ribbons. Germaine, whose restaurant in Aubrac is a temple of aligot, sees the ribbons as ties of friendship.

word *aligot* was first used in the monastery of Aubrac, now reduced to just a church, a few shattered walls and the bell that used to toll to summon back any pilgrims who might have lost their way.

When the north wind « Ecir » joined forces with the snow, the only hope for pilgrims was the hospitality of the monks. It was a tradition that travelers would always receive something (« quelque chose ») to eat at the abbey's gate. « Something » is *aliquid* in Latin, *aliquod* in medieval Latin, and *aligot* in Occitane. Before Parmentier introduced potatoes to France, this « something » must have been bread topped with a little melted *tomme* as a simple refreshment to substitute for a home-cooked meal.

The word comes from Aubrac, but this rustic meal can be found beyond the plateau where it originated. It is a dish of all the mountain people. François Rongier, a true native of Cantal, was not satisfied with preparing one of the best *truffades* of the region in his chalet in the Col de Serre; he also makes *patranque*, a dish which all the older residents of Cantal believe really originated here. Historians discern its traces as far back as 1000 A.D.

Patranque consists of cubes of rye bread rubbed with garlic and toasted in an oven with *tomme* added at the end. *Aligot* and *truffade* thus share a common ancestor. One legend leads to another, and natives of Cantal like to tell how Aurillac's native son, crowned Pope Gerbert, was served *patranque* accompanied by gingered ham at the feast held in his honor.

Aligot, truffade…variations on the same ingredients, just as there are different versions of shared stories. « You can determine the region for each dish from the countryside itself, » states Louis-Jacques Liandier, a novelist who is mayor of Vic-sur-Cère. « It's *truffade* where you find the cattle of Salers, and it's *aligot* where the Aubrac breed grazes. »

« Truffade *and* aligot *both form ribbons and they both bring together tablefuls of happy people.* »

The cows of Salers have red coats, Aubracs are wheat-colored, and both have huge eyes and lyre shaped horns. They have their own pedigrees and classifications, but they are cousins in spirit if not in blood. Both breeds are sure footed, with a certain wild streak. They share an intense maternal instinct and tolerate being milked only if their calf is standing by their side. Milk from the Aubracs is used to make laguiole, which bears a strong resemblance to the cantal and salers made from the red cows' milk.

Aligot at every celebration

Rooted in their homelands, *truffade* and *aligot* compete with the famous pocketknives made in Languiole for popular affection. Auvergnats went up to Paris en masse after World War I, and the capital became familiar with the dishes they prepared for themselves in the backrooms behind the counters of their coal and firewood shops, which gradually became neighborhood bistros. *Aligots* and *truffades* were as evocative for the homesick Auvergnats as *madeleines* were for Proust. The dishes were savored at banquets in Paris where every guest seated at the table hailed from the same village. Aubrac became a mythic spot where these exiles returned each summer to follow « whey cures » and to consume *aligot*, reputed to « restore tired stomachs.» Once nothing more than a crossroads in front of the abbey, the village developed into a little vacation center.

The tradition continues today. In her restaurant in Aubrac, Madame Germaine transforms the service of *aligot* into a sort of baptismal rite, christening the celebrants with a generous tonsure of grated cheese and commemorating this rite with a certificate. Tourists and sightseers flock to the spot, and *aligot* has become a local attraction. The dish's popularity reached a new level in the 1960s when the cooperative « Jeune Montagne » in Laguiole used *aligot* as a marketing ploy in its campaign to preserve local cheese-making. « We delivered free *tommes fraîches* to associations and local committees who wanted to organize festivals around an enormous *aligot*, » recalls André Valadier, the cooperative's president. « The promotion was such a success that we couldn't keep it up. We had to start billing for our products. » A big local celebration is now unimaginable without a vast cauldron where attendees enjoy stirring and spinning an *aligot* into thick ribbons. In 1983, the cooperative began to produce frozen *aligot* and now sells up two million portions annually throughout France and abroad.

Aligot and *truffade* are flourishing. You will find them on the most fashionable, as well as proletarian, tables. It is not by chance that Michel Bras, whose Michelin three-star restaurant dominates the Languiole plateau, has his own mother stirring a pot of *aligot* every day. A sample is sent out to each diner, with the chef's compliments. It is an extra bonus that comes from the heart and a reverence for tradition.

Le « voyage de l'aligot » de Michel Bras

In his three-star restaurant overlooking the Laguiole plateau, Michel Bras offers an « *aligot* journey » beginning in the year 1000 with rye bread and cheese and concluding in 2000 with a delicacy that is an elegant marriage of the flavors of potatoes and walnuts.

1- Cut the bread into small pieces, and soak them in the milk for 1 hour. Peel the potatoes, cut them up into small pieces and steam them for 10 to 15 minutes.
2- Cut the *tomme* into small dice, squeeze out the bread, and combine it with the *tomme* and rye flour to make the dough smooth. Season with salt and pepper.
3- Heat the peanut oil in a non-stick pan. Form the dough into 6 pancakes, each about 3/4-inch thick and 2 1/2-inches in diameter. Cook them one at a time over low heat for about 3 minutes to very lightly brown one side and flip gently with a spatula. The center of the pancakes should remain very soft and the outside should be crunchy. Set them aside and keep them warm.
4- Whip the cream. Mash the potatoes with the butter in a manual food press. Carefully combine the potato puree with the whipped cream. Season with salt and pepper.
5- Place the pancakes on individual serving plates. Form the potato puree into 6 ovals and place one on each pancake. Sprinkle with chopped walnuts and drizzle each dish with walnut oil.
Serve with a small salad as a first course.

Serves 6
Preparation time : 35 minutes
Soaking time : 1 hour
Cooking : 50 minutes

14 oz. slightly stale sour dough bread
14 oz. fresh *tomme de Laguiole*
1 lb., 12 oz. potatoes
5 1/4 oz. liquid *crème fraîche*, very cold
6 3/4 oz. milk
1 ounce butter
1 3/4 oz. walnut oil
3 1/2 oz. peanut oil
2 teaspoons rye flour
4 1/4 oz. walnut meats
salt and pepper

La patranque du Col de Serre

François Rongier, a native son of Cantal, prepares a delectable *patranque* in his chalet in the Col de Serre. A forbear of *truffade*, *patranque* is truly a local dish. You simply replace the potatoes with pieces of slightly stale country bread.

1- Cut up the country bread into large cubes and brown them in a pan with the melted butter. Drain the bread on absorbent paper towels. Cut the garlic cloves in half and rub them over the croutons. Arrange the croutons in an earthenware cooking plate and keep them warm.
2- Wash and chop the parsley.
Pour the *crème fraîche* into a small pot and warm it for 2 minutes. Add the *tomme* cut up into small pieces and stir gently.
When the cheese begins to melt (like a *fondue*), add a pinch of salt and pepper and pour the cream and cheese mixture over the croutons. Sprinkle with parsley and serve immediately.

Serves 4
Preparation time : 20 minutes
Cooking time : 20 minutes

1 lb., 5 oz. country bread
14 oz. *tomme fraîche*
2 3/4 oz. butter
3 1/2 oz. *crème fraîche*
2 garlic cloves
1/2 bunch parsley
salt and pepper

the center

Potée in the Auvergne

Potées are served all over France; what could be simpler than putting vegetables and meat together in a stewpot? Cabbage, carrots, potatoes, and salted pork are used here. We think of *potée* as Auvergnat in its origins, perhaps because it takes us back to the earliest history of the tribes of the region. Vercingetorix himself was a fan of the dish.

Above
Winter in the Auvergne: the art of living.

Facing page
Cabbages are left out in kitchen gardens until the first snowfall.

Potée is a meal for those snowy winters, storm-tossed by the bitterly cold wind called the « Ecir ». The « Traversée blanche » was a weeklong journey on horseback across a mountainous chain of extinct volcanoes from southern to northern Auvergne. The route crossed the Limon plateau, one of the most barren, desolate highlands in Cantal, with fences as the only guideposts. The journey was a test of endurance undertaken by pilgrims and peddlers even in the harshest winters. To fortify these travelers 100 years ago, a huge cauldron called an « ola » was set up on a tripod in the inner courtyard of a barn near Murat. The vessel was a battered smelting pot from the foundries at Rosières, a forgotten relic quietly ending its career in the wind and the rain, usually cooking potatoes for the pigs. Beginning early in the morning, men stoked the fire under the tripod, and put cabbage, potatoes, turnips, leeks, and carrots on to simmer, all vegetables that stick to the ribs. They did not stint with the salted meat, the pork belly, and the ham hocks. At last, another symbol emerged from the clouds of savory steam: a nationally honored dish, the mightily restorative *potée auvergnate*.

In the beginning was the pot

Potée is actually no more Auvergnat than it is Breton or Lorraine. Every province in France has conceived the notion of putting garden vegetables « into the pot » and seasoning them with a few pieces of pork, a meat which used to be salted and kept year round in farm cellars. It is a mistake to assume that *pot-au-feu* is a dish of boiled beef; you will find *pots-au-feu* made with pork, chicken, and even fish, depending on the location. In the beginning, there was simply a pot, some water, a fire, and the pot heating over the fire. The work *potage* designated any hearty dish of meat and vegetables boiled together, as this inimitable verse by Boileau attests: « Then they served forth a soup / And a rooster was there with a splendid retinue »…

> « *The* potée *family is large, and related to the* pot-au-feu *family, which is larger still.* »

A *potée* is really just a hearty soup, a variation on *pot-au-feu* with braised salted pork and cabbage as the primary ingredients. This combination resonates with history. Cabbage and pork are almost the quintessence of the Gallic identity, and the Gallic identity (they refer to it as « Arverne » in these parts) is the Auvergnat identity. This is the sense of nationhood honored all around Clermont-Ferrand, in the ruins of the legendary Gergovie, and at the summit of Puy de Dôme, the Celtic Mount Olympus, where that most powerful of gods Teutates was once worshipped.

La potée auvergnate

Serves 6
Preparation time : 20 minutes
Soaking time : 12 hours
Cooking time : 3 hours 30 minutes

1 heel end of smoked ham,
weighing 7 oz.
1 salted pig's knuckle
10 1/2 oz. bacon
6 Auvergne style sausages
1 green cabbage
3 carrots
1 large *kohlrabi*
3 turnips
12 potatoes
1 leek
1 *bouquet garni*
peppercorns

This is the classic recipe for *potée auvergnate*, which calls for adding garden vegetables to the pot and requires hours of slow simmering.

1- The day before you prepare the dish, soak the ham and pig's knuckle 12 hours, changing the water every 3 hours.
2- Combine the ham, pig's knuckle, bacon, and *bouquet garni* in a stew pot. Pour over 3 quarts of water and simmer the meat 2 hours over low heat.
3- Peel and wash the vegetables. Cut them up into large pieces and add them to the stew pot together with the sausages and a few peppercorns. Place the potatoes on top. Continue to cook over low heat for another 1 1/2 hours. When the meat and vegetables are tender, correct the seasoning and remove from heat.
4- Serve the *potée* as two courses, first the broth and then the meat and vegetables.

La soupe au chou

Serves 6
Preparation time : 30 minutes
Soaking time : 12 hours
Cooking time : 2 hours 25 minutes

1 small green cabbage
2 onions, peeled
12 potatoes
2 carrots
3 turnips
6 thin slices of salted bacon
2 Auvergne style sausages
2 cloves
1 *bouquet garni*
2 3/4 oz. butter
6 slices rye bread
salt and pepper

Potée is really a hearty soup, and *soupe au chou* is basically a *potée* with extra broth.

1- The day before you prepare the dish, soak the bacon slices in cold water, changing the water every 3 hours.
2- Place the sausages and the bacon slices in a soup pot, together with the onions, each stuck with a clove. Pour over 2 quarts of water and simmer the meats 1 hour over low heat, skimming occasionally.
3- Cut the cabbage into quarters. Peel and cut the carrots and turnips into large regular pieces. Add these vegetables to the soup pot together with the *bouquet garni* and cook for 1 additional hour.
4- Peel the potatoes. Cut them into large cubes and add them to the broth on top of the other vegetables. Continue cooking 20 minutes more, always over low heat.
Meanwhile, melt the butter in a large skillet. Cook the bread slices in the foaming butter, browning on all sides.
5- Remove the soup pot from the heat. Drain the sausages and the bacon and cut them into pieces. Correct the seasoning of the broth. Place a slice of bread in each bowl. Arrange the meat on top and pour the broth over all. Serve piping hot.

Caesar was astonished by the countless swine that wandered freely around villages searching for acorns. The Gauls were experts in preserving meat in brine and rapidly became known as skilled *charcutiers*. After the battle of Alésia, the Romans provisioned themselves with ham and bacon from the Gauls. Cabbage was also a barbarian specialty, and its very name in both French and English is derived from the Celtic *kep*. When Gergovie was under siege and an entire nation was riveted by Arverne resistance, it is more than likely that Vercingetorix must have fantasized about a *potée*. With cabbage and salted pork as its basic ingredients, his dish would have strongly resembled the one that makes the mouth of a displaced Auvergnat water even today, as he stands behind the bar of his bistro in Paris.

An everyday dish, born of necessity

Potée takes us back to a legendary ancient golden age. It also brings recollections of more recent times, when a simple, yet reassuringly stable, rural economy flourished. It was an era when preserving food for the winter was essential, when men and livestock lived under the same roof. A *saigneur* (professional hog butcher) orchestrated the ritual of pig slaughtering at the beginning of winter. This was a time when people didn't have to scrimp and save. The *potée* was left to simmer three or four hours in its cauldron, set in a *cantou*, a fireplace so enormous that ancestors would sit on a bench in a corner within to get warmer. The bubbling of the stew was background music for their conversations.

At Coltines on the Planèze plateau in the department of Cantal, there is not a single tree to break the wind, and the soil is so poor that, until the miracle of fertil-izers, people could grow nothing but lentils, another local specialty. The granite houses here have walls that are two meters thick, and the kitchen, where the entire family lived, opened directly into the stables. The pig had winter quarters next to the cows; he was sheltered there during those bitterly cold months so that he too could share a little warmth with the other animals. The root cellar lay behind, where cabbages, potatoes, and carrots were kept on a bed of sand. The stone salting tub for preserving meats stood nearby. Like *potée* itself, this architecture narrates the story of a whole way of life in its own language.

A whole menu in just one dish

A number of other treasures of Auvergnat cooking are structured around this same *potée*. We could begin with the legendary *soupe aux choux*. *Potée* can provide not only the main course, but the appetizer as well.

« *The best* potée *is made just after the pig is slaughtered. When the meat has been salted four or five days, it takes on a distinctive flavor, but it's still fresh.* »

In this commonsense part of the world, a broth savory with meat and vegetables is not allowed to go to waste. It is ladled over a few slices of rye bread, and there is nothing to prevent you from adding a few cabbage leaves to give the soup some body. Is the *potée* more than you can finish tonight? The leftovers can be used to prepare stuffed cabbage the next day. All you have to do is blanch some nice fresh cabbage leaves, and last night's *potée* will give you the tastiest stuffing you can imagine. François Rongier started out serving drinks in a Parisian cafe before returning home to open a restaurant in the Col de Serre amidst the extinct volcanoes of Cantal. « If you want to prepare a real *choux farcis*, you have to start with a *potée*, » he explains. « If you can moisten the dish when it's baking in the oven with a little broth from the same *potée*, it turns out even better. » *Potée* is a theme on which you can play as many variations as an Auvergnat winter has moods.

Le chou farci

In this stuffed cabbage recipe, you will find the same ingredients used in *potée* and *soupe au chou*, but here they are chopped, wrapped in cabbage leaves and braised. The Auvergne has many recipes for stuffed cabbage; this preparation may be served hot or chilled like a *pâté* or *terrine*.

Serves 6 to 8
Preparation time : 1 hour 30 minutes
Cooking time : 2 hours 10 minutes

1 green cabbage
10 1/2 oz.salted pig's knuckle
2 egg whites
8 1/2 oz. liquid *crème fraîche*
8 3/4 oz. sausage meat
salt and pepper

1- Immerse the whole cabbage in a large pot of boiling water for 7 or 8 minutes. Refresh it under cold water and drain it, carefully removing the core without detaching the leaves.
2- Cut up the meat from the pig's knuckle and blend it with the egg whites in a food processor. Season with salt and pepper. Add the *crème fraîche* and the sausage meat. Continue to blend until the stuffing is smooth.
3- Gently strip the leaves from the cabbage until you get to its heart. Remove the heart carefully and cut it in half. Chop one of the halves. Add the chopped cabbage heart to the stuffing, mixing it thoroughly. Put the stuffing into the cabbage. Fold the leaves up one by one, overlapping them to make the cabbage its original shape.
4- Spread out a dampened dishtowel on a working surface. Lay 4 lengths of string underneath it in a star-shaped pattern. Place the cabbage in the center of the towel. Fold the corners of the towel up to cover the cabbage completely and pull them together very tightly. Knot the strings together on top.
5- Immerse the cabbage in a large soup pot filled with salted water and cook 2 hours over low heat. Drain thoroughly and serve very hot.

La potée de chou et haddock

This cabbage soup recipe is prepared with smoked pork and fish.

Serves 6
Preparation time : 30 minutes
Cooking time : 2 hours

1 small Savoy cabbage
2 carrots
3 potatoes
3 turnips
1 onion
3 thin slices of *coppa* (a Corsican ham)
14 oz. haddock
2 quarts chicken bouillon (You may use bouillon cubes.)
1 *bouquet garni*
1 3/4 oz. butter
salt and pepper

1- Peel the carrots and turnips. Wash the cabbage and cut it up into 6 large pieces. Chop the onion.
2- Melt the butter in a pot and sauté the chopped onion without letting it brown. Add the *coppa*, the cabbage, the carrots, and the turnips. Cook 5 minutes, then pour over the bouillon and add the *bouquet garni*. Let the soup simmer over low heat for about 1 1/2 hours.
3- 25 minutes before you are ready to serve, add the haddock, cut up into thick pieces, and the peeled potatoes to the pot. Cook an additional 20 minutes over low heat.
4- Serve the *potée* piping hot in deep bowls. You may enjoy it as the residents of Cantal do, with thick slices of toasted bread rubbed with garlic.

Burgundy

Les gougères

Serves 6

Preparation time : 15 minutes

Cooking time : 30 minutes

4 oz. water
4 1/2 oz. flour
3 1/2 oz. butter, plus 1/2 oz. for greasing the pastry tray
4 eggs
7 3/4 oz. gruyère
pinch of salt

1- Heat the water, salt, and butter together in a large pot. When it comes to the boiling point, pour in the flour all at once, stirring vigorously. The dough should not cook; it should form into a ball that pulls away from the sides of the pot. Remove from the heat. Fold in 3 1/2 oz. of the gruyère, finely diced, then the eggs one at a time, stirring with a wooden spatula.
2- With a large spoon or scoop, shape small amounts of the dough the size of a large walnut, and set them on a buttered pastry tray.
3- Sprinkle them with the remaining cheese, grated, and bake them 30 minutes at 340°. When the *gougères* are browned and puffy, serve them hot as *hors d'oeuvres* with a bottle of *crémant de Bourgogne*.

Les œufs meurette

Serves 6

Preparation time : 25 minutes

Cooking time : 40 minutes

6 eggs
17 oz. red wine, plus 8 1/2 oz. for poaching the eggs
7 oz. veal stock (You also may use freeze dried veal stock.)
1 large onion, chopped
1 garlic clove, crushed in its skin
1 3/4 oz. butter
8 3/4 oz. bacon
1/2 oz. flour
6 slices of bread
1 *bouquet garni*
2 sprigs of parsley
salt and pepper

1- Sauté the onion and the bacon until lightly browned. Add the flour and mix with a wooden spatula.
2- Pour over the veal stock and reduce by half. Add the garlic and its skin, the *bouquet garni*, the red wine, and 3 cups of water. Season with salt and pepper and simmer 20 minutes over low heat. Remove the *bouquet garni*.
3- Bring the remaining wine to a simmer. Break the eggs into individual ramekins and poach them one by one in the simmering wine.
4- Toast the bread slices.
5- Place each egg on a slice of toast, together with the bacon and onion mixture. Arrange the toasts on a service platter and cover with the red wine sauce. Garnish with the chopped parsley and serve very hot.

Lyonnais

La cervelle de canut

A recipe from Le Jura in Lyon

Serves 6

Preparation time : 10 minutes

4 *fromages blancs en faisselle* (soft white cheese)
1/4 of a fresh goat cheese
2 tablespoons thick *crème fraiche*
1 tablespoon dry white wine
2 shallots
1 bunch chives
1 small bunch parsley
2 tablespoons olive oil
salt, freshly ground pepper and cayenne pepper

1- Chop the shallots and the parsley finely. Slice the chives.
2- Whisk the *fromages blancs* together with the *crème fraiche*. Add the goat cheese, the wine, the olive oil, and the herbs. Season with salt and pepper.
3- You may serve this dish cold with *crudités* or with warm boiled potatoes in their jackets. It may also be served with toast at the end of a meal in place of a cheese course.

La salade de pommes de terre et saucisson chaud à la pistache façon « coco »

Serves 6

Preparation time : 30 minutes

Cooking time : 20 minutes

1 uncooked sausage with pistachio nuts
12 new potatoes
2 shallots
4 tablespoons peanut oil
2 tablespoons wine vinegar
1 *bouquet garni*
fleur de sel (flaky sea salt) and freshly ground pepper

1- Wash the potatoes and peel them. Cook them for 20 minutes in boiling water with the sausage and *bouquet garni*.
2- Peel and finely chop the shallots. Combine the oil, the vinegar, and the shallots. Season with salt and pepper.
3- Drain the potatoes. Cut them into thick rounds and arrange them on plates. While they are still warm, cover them with the vinaigrette.
4- Cut the sausage into thick slices. Add the sausage pieces to the potatoes. Season with *fleur de sel* and pepper. Serve the dish very hot.

Les bugnes

Makes 25 *bugnes*

Preparation time : 15 minutes

Cooking time : 25 minutes

6 oz. flour
1 3/4 oz. butter, softened
2 eggs
1/2 tsp. baking powder
zest of 1 lemon
! teaspoon rum
1 teaspoon granulated sugar
1 tablespoon confectioners' sugar
deep fryer

1- Combine the flour, eggs, granulated sugar, and baking powder in a large bowl. Add the butter, lemon zest, and rum. Mix with your fingertips until the dough is smooth. Roll it out very thin.
2- Cut the dough up into 4-inch triangles, using a pastry cutter.
3- Heat the oil in the deep fryer. When the oil is very hot, immerse several pieces of the dough. When they rise to the surface, continue cooking them until they are nicely browned. Remove them with a skimmer and lay them on paper towels to drain. Continue frying the *bugnes* until you have used all the dough.
4- Arrange on a serving plate, sprinkle with confectioners' sugar and eat while they are still warm.

Sologne

Le brochet au bleu

Serves 6 to 8
Preparation time : 50 minutes
Cooking time : 50 minutes

2 pike, weighing 3 1/2 lbs. each
3 carrots
3 onions
10 1/2 oz. butter, cut in small pieces
1 tablespoon *liquid crème* fraîche
17 oz. white wine vinegar
1 large *bouquet garni*
15 peppercorns
2 cloves
1 1/2 oz. coarse salt

1- Peel the vegetables and cut them into very thin rounds. Cook them in 4 quarts boiling water with the *bouquet garni*, cloves, and salt for 20 minutes.
2- Clean the fish. Place them on the rack of a fish poacher and sprinkle them with the vinegar. Pour the hot *court bouillon* over the fish. (They will immediately arch back.) Cover and simmer 20 to 30 minutes. Remove from heat. Slide the pike carefully onto a serving platter and keep warm.
3- In a small pot, bring a ladle of the bouillon and the *crème fraîche* to the boiling point. Remove from heat, and carefully whisk in the butter, piece by piece. Serve the fish with the butter sauce.

Limousin

Le pâté limousin

Serves 6
Preparation time : 55 minutes
Resting time : 40 minutes
Cooking time : 45 minutes

1 lb. large potatoes
6 garlic cloves
1 small bunch Italian parsley, chopped
10 1/2 oz. sausage meat
6 3/4 oz. *crème fraîche*
salt and pepper

For the pastry
18 oz. flour,
plus 13/4 oz. for the pan
4 eggs, plus 1 yolk for glazing
2 tablespoons duck fat
1 ounce baker's yeast
pinch of sugar
pinch of salt

1- Peel and cut the potatoes in slices 1-inch thick. Peel and mince the garlic.
2- In a large bowl, combine the flour, yeast, salt, sugar, duck fat and 4 eggs and mix with your fingertips. Cover the dough with a damp cloth and let it rise 40 minutes at room temperature. In a shallow bowl, combine the potatoes, *crème fraîche*, sausage meat, garlic, and chopped parsley. Season with salt and pepper.
3- Preheat the oven to 350°. Roll out the pastry 1-inch thick and divide it in half. Place one piece into a floured baking dish. Put the potato-sausage mixture on top. Fold the edges toward the center, then place the other sheet of dough on top.
4- Brush the dough with the beaten egg yolk. Arrange decoratively cut out scraps of dough on top. Moisten the edges of the dough with water, then seal between your thumb and index finger. Cut a small hole in the top and insert a little « chimney » of greaseproof paper to allow steam to escape. Bake the pastry 45 minutes at 340°. Allow the pastry to cool before you slice it.

Aveyron

Les tripoux de Laguiole

Serves 6
Preparation time : 45 minutes
Cooking time : about 8 hours

8 1/2 lbs. calf's caul
2 lbs. *poches de veau**
18 oz. bacon
1 1/2 quarts beef bouillon (You may use bouillon cubes.)
8 1/2 oz. white wine
5 oz. Cognac
1 bunch of parsley
1 bunch of chives
2 onions
2 garlic cloves
1 clove
coarse salt, regular salt, freshly ground pepper
pinch of cayenne pepper

1- Blanch the calf's caul in boiling salted water. Drain and rinse under cold water. Cut it up with a knife.
2- Combine 10 1/2 oz. of the bacon, the parsley, the chives, 1 onion coarsely cut up, and the garlic and blend in a food processor. Add the chopped calf's caul and blend again until the mixture is finely and evenly chopped. Season with salt, cayenne, and pepper.
3- Cut the *poche de veau* into 12 pieces like veal scallops, each about 3-inches in diameter. Lay the veal pieces out on a work surface and top each with an equal amount of the stuffing. Fold the meat over the stuffing and sew each *tripou* closed with white linen thread.
4- Cook the *tripoux* in the bouillon with the remaining bacon left in one piece, the white wine, the Cognac, and the remaining onion with the clove stuck into it. Serve the *tripoux* very hot, moistened with their cooking juices and accompanied by steamed potatoes.

*Poche de veau is an important cut of meat in the preparation of *tripoux*, and can be purchased from local butchers in Aveyron. You may substitute very thin veal scallops.

The Southeast

Bouillabaisse in Marseille

It started as a snack for the fishermen of Marseille. Today *bouillabaisse* is one of the best known French specialties in the world. We return to the rocky inlets, the Corniche and the Vieux Port where the legend began.

Above
The fish in a bouillabaisse should be as varied as possible, but all are rock fish with a very distinctive flavor.

Facing page
Returning from a day of fishing. Tucked away in rocky inlets are many little harbors that are an integral part of the city of Marseille.

On the outskirts of the city, the street changes abruptly into a twisting road that skirts the sea. Fishermen balance on rocks, swimmers search for a stairway leading down to the water, and gulls swoop around the fishing nets with their laughing cries. Our next stop is the village of les Goudes, where cottages crowd together on flat white rocks overlooking the dark blue sea. Tourists mill about, and sailboats and speedboats bob at their moorings. One or two real fishermen still follow their fathers' trade, setting out in wooden boats with old diesel engines. There is a bakery, a church, and the « Grand Bar des Goudes » where Gaby presides on *bouillabaisse* days.

A broth concocted from sunlight

Fernandel said it all in his song: « To make a fine *bouillabaisse*, you have to be an early riser... » The work begins when the fishermen arrive with their baskets, because a great *bouillabaisse* begins with an abundant variety of rock fish, which thrive along the white limestone shore like the people here. The fish must be netted in the traditional way so they retain all their flavor, not in a trawling net, a method that drowns the fish. « It's a dying profession, » mourns Jacky, one of the last fishermen remaining in les Goudes, « because you have to maneuver very close to the reefs and you often lose your nets there. »

| « You can't make a bouillabaisse *for just two or three people. The more there are to serve, the more you can add different varieties of fish, and the better the* bouillabaisse *is.* »

Each vividly colored fish is unique: red, green or glistening blue. Gaby relishes calling each one by its name, as if reciting a litany, already tasting them as he speaks: *rascasse blanche, rascasse rouge, fielas, baudroie, saint-pierre, araignées, moustelle, chapon* (a variety of *rascasse*). In les Goudes, and only in les Goudes (other neighborhoods in Marseille do not share this tradition), they also toss in octopus, mussels and even sea urchins, which are added at the last moment to intensify the flavor.

That is how this dish must be prepared; you can't skimp on it. A *bouillabaisse* must be generous, the center piece

La bouillabaisse de poissons à la marseillaise

Serves 10
Preparation : 1 hour 30 minutes
Cooking time : about 20 minutes

9 lbs. fish and shellfish (In Marseille, the selection might include *grondin, racasse, rouget grondin*, eel, monkfish, John Dory, octopus, and spider crabs)
10 sea urchins
2 lbs., 3 oz. potatoes, peeled and cut into large pieces
7 garlic cloves
3 onions, peeled and chopped
5 very ripe tomatoes, seeded, peeled and diced
1 cup olive oil
1 *bouquet garni*
1 fennel stalk
8 threads of saffron
10 slices country style bread
salt and cayenne pepper

For the *rouille*
1 egg yolk
2 garlic cloves
1 cup olive oil
10 saffron threads
coarse salt and cayenne pepper

Here is the classic recipe for *bouillabaisse*, as prepared by Gaby, the cook in the Grand Bar des Goudes.

1- Scale and remove the fins from the fish and wash them, preferably in sea water. Cut into large pieces, leaving the bones in. Wash the octopus and cut into pieces.
2- In a large pot, heat the olive oil. Add the onions, 6 cloves of the garlic, crushed, the octopus, and the diced tomatoes. Cook over low heat for 5 minutes, stirring gently so that the oil absorbs the flavors.
3- Add the fish to the pot, beginning with the largest pieces and ending with the smallest. Cover with boiling water to deglaze the pot. Season with salt and cayenne pepper, and add the fennel, the *bouquet garni*, and the saffron. Boil over medium heat for 10 minutes, stirring gently from time to time to prevent the fish from sticking to the bottom of the pot. Correct the seasoning of the broth. The *bouillabaisse* is ready when the oil and water in the cooking juices blend together, thickening slightly.
4- Prepare the *rouille*. Peel the garlic and mash it with coarse salt in a mortar. Add the egg yolk and saffron, season with the cayenne, and whisk in the oil little by little as you would for a mayonnaise, stirring with the pestle.
5- Cook the potatoes in boiling salted water for 15 to 20 minutes. Cut open the sea urchins with scissors and scoop out the « coral » inside with a small spoon.
6- Arrange the fish on a serving platter. Add the sea urchin coral to the bouillon, stirring.
Serve the bouillon very hot in deep soup bowls, pouring it over thick slices of country style bread rubbed with garlic, accompanied by the *rouille*. Then present the fish and potatoes for guests to help themselves.

of a table so big you lose track of how many guests are seated around it. About 11:00, people start gathering at the bar, savoring a first Ricard, which usually calls for a chaser. Conversations grow livelier. Although the *bouillabaisse* quickly disappears, the real pleasure lies in discussing it after the meal is over.

Birth of a legend

The same scene is enacted elsewhere in the city at the same time, perhaps in Estaque, the village at the opposite side of the bay where a few men still ply the fisherman's trade, or in a little house in Sormiou. *Bouillabaisse* is a dish that is a ritual for its devotees, and its devotees are legion.

The concept of the dish goes back to the basics of the fisherman's trade. Like his Phoenician forebears, a Marseille fisherman reached his fishing grounds by sailing or rowing a considerable distance. Since the trip took three or four hours, he had to bring a snack along or find something there. Eating fish intended for sale was out of the question; the fishermen only had a claim on the *suces*, fish that had been attacked and bitten by their fellow creatures. The fishermen would cook these over a wood fire in a cauldron filled with sea water, adding garlic, which was easy to bring along, and freshly picked wild fennel. Tomatoes came later, emigrating from Central American in the seventeenth century; saffron arrived later still, a luxury that came from trade with France's eastern colonies. At this point, *bouillabaisse* was nothing more than seasoned fish broth. « The turning point came in the nineteenth century when overseas trade led to the evolution of a middle class who moved inland, » explains Monsieur Minguella, the owner of Miramar, the finest restaurant in the Vieux Port. « They hired former fishermen as cooks, who in turn introduced *bouillabaisse* to their bosses, adapting it to more sophisticated tastes. Sea water was replaced by a fish soup cooked in advance. » Thus the « real » *bouillabaisse* was invented, poised to conquer the world.

The leisure class follows the workers' example

During the Belle Époque, Marseille dreamed of becoming a fashionable seaside resort. There was dancing every evening at the Casino de la Plage. The Corniche was still just a little road along the shore, lined with whimsical follies. Chateaux and villas took on the airs of Italian or Moorish palaces. Locals made sure to serve *bouillabaisse* to their temporary guests. Once the dish of humble fishermen, *bouillabaisse* became a symbol of chic. By the end of World War II, there was not a single restaurant in the Vieux Port that did not list *bouillabaisse* on its menu.

> « *Do you know why we put leeks in* bouillabaisse*? Because they're a sovereign remedy for rheumatism. Believe me, it's absolutely true.* »

Ambrogiani, the most expressive of the city's artists, made a specialty of painting *bouillabaisse* still lifes featuring confused compositions of *rascasses* and *saint-pierres*. A short distance away, beneath the Corniche viaduct that sweeps around the little valley of Auffes, Fonfon was also hard at work for the sake of posterity. He had a quick tongue and good taste. An artist in the kitchen, he welcomed all the stars of the era as equals: Brigitte Bardot, Alain Delon, Jean Cocteau. These ambassadors bore the legend of *bouillabaisse* up to Paris. Fonfon is dead, and his nephew has tried to do everything he can to fill his uncle's shoes. The issue of *bouillabaisse*, however, has assumed a different order of magnitude: you have only to type the word on the Internet to get hundreds of hits. There are *bouillabaisses* from America, Finland, Russia; all the term really means now is a crude way of boiling everything together. In Marseille, however, everyone realizes how difficult it is to follow the recipe carefully to evoke the true spirit of the dish: you have to add the fish in order, one variety at a time, and when it starts to boil (*bouille*), you lower (*baisse*) the heat.

La bouillabaisse d'œufs

Serves 4
Preparation time : 25 minutes
Cooking time : 40 minutes

4 eggs
1 onion
2 leeks, white part only
2 tomatoes
8 small potatoes
4 garlic cloves
4 tablespoons olive oil
juice of 1 orange
1 *bouquet garni*
8 saffron threads
5 sprigs Italian parsley
4 slices country-style bread, toasted
fleur de sel and freshly ground pepper.

The word *bouillabaisse* is a contraction of *bouillir* (boil) and *abaisser* (lower). It is actually more descriptive of a general cooking technique than an actual recipe for fish. You may cook snails, spinach or chard in the same way.

1- Chop the onion and the white parts of the leeks. Seed the tomatoes and cut them into small pieces. Peel and cut the potatoes into very thin slices (about 1 1/2-inches thick).
2- In a large pot, warm 3 tablespoons of the olive oil. Add the onions and leeks and cook them over low heat without allowing them to take on color. Add the tomatoes, 3 garlic cloves, peeled and crushed, the orange juice, the saffron, the *bouquet garni*, the parsley, the potato slices and enough cold water to cover these ingredients by 4-inches. Season with salt and pepper and cook 20 minutes over very low heat.
3- Strain the bouillon into a pot. Set aside the vegetables and potatoes. Place the toasted bread, lightly brushed with olive oil and rubbed with garlic, into deep soup bowls. Poach the eggs in the simmering bouillon and arrange them on top of the toast slices.
4- Strain the bouillon again and add the vegetables and potatoes. Serve the bouillon and vegetables very hot together with the eggs.

La bouillabaisse de volaille et langouste

Here is a tasty *bouillabaisse* that combines the flavors of two delicious, savory ingredients: chicken and crayfish.

1- Plunge the crayfish into a pot of boiling water for 1 minute to kill it. Remove the head, and cut the body open lengthwise. Remove the meat with a small spoon and set it aside in a bowl. Blend the « coral » (the contents of the head) in a food processor and set aside in the refrigerator. Remove the tail and break up the shells of the head and tail with a hammer.

2- Peel and slice the shallots. Peel and crush 2 of the garlic cloves. Cut the tomatoes into large cubes. Heat half the olive oil in a pot and sauté the shells, the shallots and the garlic. Brown for 5 minutes, stirring, until the shells are lightly caramelized. Pour over the fish stock. Add the fennel and the saffron and boil 10 minutes over low heat. Cover with food wrap and allow the bouillon to steep for 4 hours at room temperature.

3- 30 minutes before serving, cook the potatoes in boiling salted water for 20 minutes.

4- In another pot, heat the rest of the oil and sauté the chicken breasts on both sides. Add the crayfish tail, the cubed tomatoes, and the broth. Simmer over low heat for 25 minutes.

5- Rub the garlic over the toast slices and place them in deep bowls. Arrange the chicken breasts, minced, and the crayfish meat, cut up into pieces, on top of the bread. Bring the cooking liquid to a boil and whisk in the coral. Cook 1 minute and strain through a sieve, then pour over each bowl. Serve very hot with the potatoes, which have been mashed with a fork. Do not serve *rouille* with this dish.

Serves 4
Preparation time : 30 minutes
Resting time : 4 hours
Cooking time : 1 hour

4 breasts of Bresse chickens
1 live crayfish weighing 5 1/2 lbs.
4 potatoes
8 saffron threads
2 tomatoes
2 shallots
3 garlic cloves
4 tablespoons olive oil
1 stalk of wild fennel
17 oz. fish stock (You may use powdered stock.)
4 slices of toasted country style bread
fleur de sel and freshly ground pepper

Le compressé de bouillabaisse de Joël Passédat

The secret of a good *compressé* is to start with an excellent *bouillabaisse*. This recipe comes from Joël Passédat, chef of the restaurant Le Petit Nice in Marseille. This dish uses *bouillabaisse à la marseillaise* as a base.

1- Remove the fish filets from the *bouillabaisse* and carefully pick out all the bones. Soften the leaves of gelatin in a bowl of cold water. Strain the bouillon and pour it into a pot. Warm the bouillon and immerse the gelatin leaves, stirring to dissolve them.

2- Spread a layer of fish in the bottom of a porcelain terrine, and cover them with the dissolved gelatin. Add the potatoes cut up into rounds, then the rest of the fish, then the bouillon. Press each layer down lightly with the back of a spoon. Put the terrine in the refrigerator to cool for 3 hours.

3- When you are ready to serve, unmould the terrine on a cutting board and cut it into thick slices with an electric knife. Serve the slices of *compressé* with *aïoli* and toasted slices of bread, which have been seasoned with salt and pepper, and lightly rubbed with oil and garlic. This dish is also delicious with a dandelion salad dressed with good olive oil.

Serves 6
Preparation time : 30 minutes
Refrigeration time : 3 hours

1 lb., 2 oz. cooked *bouillabaisse* with 10 1/2 oz. potatoes and 1 quart of bouillon
5 leaves of gelatin
5 1/4 oz. *aïoli* (see page 151)
6 slices of country-style bread
1 3/4 oz. olive oil
1 garlic clove
salt and pepper

the southeast

Fondue in Savoie

There is nothing more basic than setting a pot on the table to allow guests to do their own very simple cooking. In the land of gruyère and beaufort, this tradition has evolved into a well-established recipe, much influenced by middle-class cuisine in the nineteenth century and more recently by the tourists who flock to Savoie every winter.

Above
There is a forfeit to be paid if you drop your bread into the fondue.

Facing page
The Beaufort cooperative caves, where the cheese is aged. The cheeses must be turned and washed regularly to mature to perfection.

Picture a gala evening at Bombay's Oberoi, a grand hotel in far-away India. The establishment has selected a variation on a unique theme to fete its international guests: *fondues* for every course of the dinner, first to last. The meal begins with a *fondue chinoise* and closes with a *fondue au chocolat*. For the main course, *fondue savoyarde* is served. This anecdote does more than illustrate how the popularity of our beloved *fondue* extends far beyond the snowy horizons of French ski stations. It also gives a fresh perspective on a practice that is commonplace all over the world: setting out a platter to be shared by the whole table and inviting guests to do a little cooking on their own. You may of course offer melted cheese, but, depending on the culture, you might also provide green vegetables, onions, meat or whatever else people like to share together.

The prince of gruyères

For the last decade, Fabrice Pacton has spent his summers in the high mountain pastures of la Tarentaise in Savoie. The stone chalet that is his mountain retreat from mid-June is also a modern laboratory where he makes tommes, each one weighing some fifty kilos, every day. The herds of cattle here include Abondances, with their dark red coats and white spots, and Tarines, with their brown coats and eyes fetchingly outlined in black. Although he is not the son of a farmer or shepherd, Fabrice chose the profession of cheese making for love of these vast open spaces and his admiration for the cheese which is generally considered the prince of gruyères, with its own AOC to back it up: beaufort.

Beaufort is a mandatory ingredient in any self-respecting *fondue*. Its flavor bears some resemblance to that of cheeses made nearby, comté and emmenthal, which were imported to Savoie in the beginning of the nineteenth century by Swiss emmigrants from Berne. Each family then added its own little secret, often inspired by the cheese called *tomme de Savoie*, which absorbed a distinctive flavor from the farm where it was produced. All that is needed is a cooking pot rubbed with garlic and white wine from Apremont, Abymes or Chignin to give the mixture a

flinty edge. Stir it all together with a wooden spoon and set out all the cubes of brown bread you want. Some people toss in a few spoonfuls of Kirsch at the end, a reminder that Alsace is not so far away. The Alpine passes are not barriers at all; they have been traversed for centuries by Hannibal, by star athletes of the Tour de France, and even by humble peddlers.

Mutual assistance and sharing good times around a cheese

Cheese from Beaufort was widely consumed in the Middle Ages. In the poorest households it took the form of *sérac*, made with the whey left over from making gruyère; it was a basic ingredient, just like the pork stored in the salting tub. « Although we do not have precise numbers to measure consumption levels of cheese, we can tell from the accounts kept by convents that it grew steadily through the eighteenth century, just as butter and cream consumption did over the same period, » write Jean and Renée Nicolas in *Daily Life in Savoie in the Seventeenth and Eighteenth Centuries*. Whether made in Switzerland or France, gruyère is a pressed cheese whose curds are heated to about 122° fahrenheit to solidify them. The idea of re-heating the finished cheese over an open flame, far from being heretical, seems to be a piece of supporting evidence. After being aged, the cheese is quite firm. It would have been necessary to melt it down to make it easier to eat in an era when dental hygiene left much to be desired.

In 1477, a traveling doctor returning from Maurienne raved about cheeses as big as a man's arm. They were very rich and melted beautifully. Local people called them « nombles ». This information appears again a century later in the records of the abbey of Talloires. Pieces of cheese were often simply warmed on glowing embers. It was an evening custom that carried on uninterrupted all the way to the Belle Époque.

Savoie's social organization served to encourage this type of communal activity. The « fruitière », an early form of cheese cooperative, is evidence of an unusual systematically organized communal life in the region. Savoyards learned very early to share their pastures and production facilities. Those cheese cubes threaded onto the point of an « Opinel » (a flexible knife made in Maurienne since 1890) and toasted

Facing page, above
The Beaufort range in autumn. When the summer is over, it is time to return to the valleys.

Facing page, below
After being heated, the curds are gathered in a huge sack. They will be poured into molds.

Above, left
When the curds have been put into the molds, they are put in a cheese press.

Above, right
Washing the cloths used in cheese making is a daily task for François Bonnet. He makes beaufort all summer long in the lofty mountain retreat of La Baume.

« *Where does this recipe come from? Probably not from the Savoyard peasants. The older ones still cannot get over how anybody could waste wine by mixing it with cheese.* »

La fondue savoyarde

Preparation time : 15 minutes
Cooking time : 10 minutes
Equipment : a *fondue* set (with a glazed earthenware or enameled finish)

14 oz. aged beaufort
14 oz. fresh beaufort
2 garlic cloves
3/4 oz. Kirsch
16 oz. dry white wine (from Apremont)
pinch of ground nutmeg
salt and pepper
14 oz. rye bread

1- Cut the cheese into small dice. Slice the garlic cloves in half without peeling them and rub them over the bottom and sides of the *fondue* pot.

2- Put the cheese pieces in the pot with the white wine and melt together over low heat, stirring constantly. Keep at a slow boil for 3 minutes until the cheese and wine are completely blended.

3- Place the alcohol-fuelled heating element in the center of the table. Cut the bread into cubes and distribute them equally among your guests.

4- When you are ready to serve, pour in the Kirsch and stir to combine. Season with salt, pepper and ground nutmeg. Serve very hot with a white wine from Apremont or Myans.

La soupe crémeuse de fromage et pommes de terre au pain brûlé

This light, simple recipe combines the cheese of a *fondue* with the potatoes of a *tartiflette*.

Serves 6
Preparation time : 20 minutes
Cooking time : 55 minutes

10 1/2 oz. potatoes
1 shallot
1 leek, white part only
1 garlic clove, cut in half
7 oz. reblochon
3 1/2 oz. beaufort
5 1/4 oz. rye bread, toasted or slightly stale
1 quart chicken bouillon (You may also use bouillon cubes.)
1 3/4 oz. liquid *crème fraîche*
3 3/4 oz. butter
salt and pepper

1- Peel the potatoes and cut into large cubes. Wash and chop the leek. Peel and mince the shallot.

2- Melt 3 oz. of the butter in a pot. When it foams, sauté the leek and shallot without allowing them to take on color and let them soften for 10 minutes over low heat. Add the potato pieces. Season with salt and pepper. Pour over the chicken bouillon and cook the soup for 35 minutes.

3- Cut the bread into thick slices. Rub them with the halved garlic clove, spread them with the remaining butter, and brown under the broiler. Let the toast slices cool slightly, then grind them to crumbs in a food processor. Cut the cheese into small dice.

4- Blend the soup thoroughly in the pot. Add the *crème fraîche* and cheese, stirring constantly. Cook 5 minutes over low heat, correct the seasoning, and pour the soup into deep bowls. Sprinkle generously with bread crumbs and serve piping hot.

La tartiflette

This recipe is a more elaborate variation on fondue, with the cheese (preferably reblochon) melted on a crusty bed of potatoes and local ham.

1- Cook the unpeeled potatoes for 15 minutes in boiling salted water. Drain them and cut them into thick rounds.
2- In a frying pan, heat the butter until it foams and cook the onions until soft. Add the diced ham and the potato rounds.
3- Scrape the rind from the reblochon and cut it in half horizontally. Place the cheese on top of the potatoes.
4- Pour over the white wine and cook the *tartiflette* in a preheated 350° oven for 30 minutes. The *tartiflette* should be crusty on the outside and creamy within. Serve with a dandelion leaf salad.

Serves 6
Preparation time : 20 minutes
Cooking time : 1 hour

6 lbs. potatoes
2 large onions, peeled and chopped
1 thick slice of smoked ham (about 2 lbs.), diced
14 oz. white wine from Savoie
1 reblochon
1 3/4 oz. butter
salt and pepper

over an open hearth are just one more indication of the Savoyard proclivity for sharing.

Fondue descends from the mountains

There were soon several more sophisticated recipes in circulation. Switzerland seems to have embraced *fondue* more readily than France. In special earthenware pots called « caquelons », they would add anchovies from the Mediterranean or juice of bitter oranges from Milan. This is the recipe known as *berthoud* that you will still find in Chablais today.

The *fondue* we are familiar with seems to be most closely associated with northern Savoie, where the Swiss influence is strongest, at least among the common folk. Toward the end of the eighteenth century, well-off travelers discovered the charms of the mountains and the healthful virtues of pure air. Laying down new culinary laws, they saw to it that *fondue* made a world class national debut. It was the era when Aix-les-Bains played host to the nobility of the courts of Europe, while Lamartine waxed ecstatic over the beauties of Lac Bourget. These tourists before the fact took the opportunity to lure Savoyards down from their mountain fastnesses to cook in the kitchens of the wealthy Parisian bourgeoisie. The simple *fondue* of the old days was adapted to sophisticated soirees. Recipes for the dish henceforth resembled the one codified by Brillat-Savarin; he was well informed on the subject, since he was born in Buget, very close to Savoie. « Take one egg for each guest. Weigh them and measure 1/3 of their weight in gruyère and 1/6 of their weight in

butter. Break the eggs into a pan and beat them. Add the butter and the grated cheese. Cook, turning gently with a spatula until the mixture thickens. Add pepper. Serve with a generous amount of excellent wine. » Hardly a light dish, but very much to the taste of this gentleman in his heyday; one contemporary reported that Brillat-Savarin would enjoy a *fondue* after a few dozen oysters, a helping of broiled kidneys, and a generous portion of *foie gras*.

A symbol of winter vacations

It is revealing that the 1970s editions of *Guide gourmande de la France*, which were published by *Guide Bleu* and offered a meticulous survey of the most obscure regional specialties, make no mention of *fondue*. Then came the construction of huge winter resorts, and skiing became a sport accessible to the masses. *Fondue* was easy to prepare, and its ingredients, which could be simplified, were inexpensive. The dish became a symbol of winter vacations and of good times shared around a convivial meal. It was a logical development, since the skiers in resorts such as Courcheval and Tignes honed their skills on slopes where dairy cows grazed in the summer. Now widely associated with winter vacations, *fondue* sallied forth from its home territory to scale peaks far beyond its original range—in the Alps, of course, but also in the Pyrenees and even in the Auvergne's Massif Central. Big business embraced these developments. Moulinex, Seb and their competitors produced *fondue* sets which created a sensation at home products shows. These utensils, poised between the kitchen and the living room, seemed to offer a practical way to dispense with tedious dinner preparations. *Fondue* made its way into every household in France.

> « *We still eat plenty of* fondue *here, but only at home with close friends. Never in a restaurant.* »

It really all comes down to a question of fashion, and fashion is always reinventing itself. Consider another Savoyard dish, a specialty of the Thônes region, which is now in the spotlight. It consists of potatoes, bacon and melted reblochon cheese. At the risk of confronting dubious imitations, *tartiflette* is dethroning *fondue* in ski resorts and elsewhere.

Poulet à la crème in Bresse

Whether *poularde* or *poulet*, only poultry from Bresse rates an AOC. To take maximum advantage of its rich, tender meat, the cooks in Bresse prepare the chicken with cream. The grandparents of the three star chef Georges Blanc treated Édouard Herriot to this dish. These days the entire region devotedly embraces the cult of these birds, which are handled like precious jewels.

Above

A fine poulet de Bresse can almost be tasted with the eye. The skin should be firm, uniform in color, smooth, and perfectly clean. These are among the criteria applied at the « Glorieuses », local fairs that attract professionals and gourmets.

Facing page

There used to be gray, white, and black chickens in Bresse. Now only white chickens are eligible for the very selective AOC certification. With their blue feet, white feathers, and red crests, these patriotically colored birds are exported worldwide.

Now over 70 years old, Marcel Volailler (a name almost too good to be true for an « éleveur de volaille » or poultry farmer) can still remember his first taste of *poulet à la crème*. « I was just a little kid helping my grandmother force feed the chickens and all of a sudden one of them suffocated. It took an accident for me to actually taste one of the chickens I'd seen running around the farmyard all my life. » It has been like that for centuries here. In Bresse, people do not think of a chicken as something to look forward to at a family feast; instead, it is viewed as money in the bank. City folk pay dearly for these birds.

The chicken of kings

Henri IV relished chickens from Bresse, at the risk of offending his own Béarnais compatriots. In the nineteenth century, Brillat-Savarin anointed this fowl « the queen of the chicken of kings ». Legions of twentieth century chefs from Bresse, Lyons and beyond introduced *poulet de Bresse* into the pantheon of great French cuisine. In the 1960s it was difficult to find a photograph of Paul Bocuse without some white fowl tucked under his arm. No meal was complete at the restaurant Mère Brasier, a Lyon institution, without *poularde demi-deuil*. More recently, Georges Blanc has taken up the torch and served his *poulet à la crème*, prepared from the most traditional classic recipe, to the world's heads of state when they gathered at his restaurant. It must be acknowledged that the chef's forebears had already distinguished themselves in this field. In a family inn located near the Vonnas fairgrounds, they used to welcome poultry-raising professionals who would stop by for a meal after winding up their business dealings. The legendary Mère Blanc later took her chicken, perfectly cooked, mouthwatering, juicy, and roasted to a turn, all the way to Paris. In 1933, Curnonsky, the crowned prince of gastronomes and a close friend of Colette, wrote that Mère Blanc was « the best cook in the world.» Her grandson, the three Michelin star chef Georges Blanc, takes after her, and it seems only natural that he is chairman of the highly respected Interprofessional Association of Poultry in Bresse.

La poularde à la crème

This is a recipe made with cut up chicken, the specialty of Madame Hugon, who presides over the kitchen in the legendary Lyonnais haunt, Chez Hugon.

1- Peel and chop the onions. Melt the butter in a large cast iron pot and sauté the chicken pieces without letting them brown. Season with salt and pepper. Add the onions and the white wine and lower the heat. Cover and cook 40 minutes over very low heat, stirring occasionally.

2- Midway through the cooking time, when the white wine has almost completely evaporated, sprinkle the chicken pieces with the flour, stir to coat them, and add the *crème fraîche*. Continue cooking until done, basting the chicken pieces with the cream sauce from time to time.

3- Arrange the chicken pieces on a serving platter. Remove the pan from the heat. Add the egg yolks and whisk to incorporate. Correct the seasoning and add the lemon juice. Cover the chicken pieces with the sauce and serve with rice pilaf.

Serves 6
Preparation time : 40 minutes
Cooking time : 40 minutes

1 Bresse chicken, weighing about 2 1/2 lbs., cut up into 6 pieces
3 1/2 oz. butter
10 1/2 oz. thick *crème fraîche*
2 large onions
1 ounce flour
2 egg yolks
1 3/4 oz. white wine
juice of 1 lemon
salt and freshly ground pepper

La poularde de Bresse aux échalotes confites en cocotte lutée

A chicken from Bresse is delicious simply roasted or prepared *en cocotte* with shallots. Make sure the casserole is hermetically sealed to lock in all the flavor.

1- Place the *bouquets garnis* into the cavity of the chicken and truss it. Season with salt and pepper. Preheat the oven to 340°.

2- Wash the shallots and garlic cloves, but do not peel them. Place the chicken in a cast iron or Pyrex casserole. Arrange the whole shallots and garlic cloves around it. Place the bacon pieces over the breast of the chicken. Season with salt and pepper, and sprinkle the chicken and its seasonings with olive oil. Cover the casserole.

3- Seal the top hermetically with a wide strip of the pastry. Beat the egg yolk in a bowl with 2 tablespoons of water. Use a brush to apply the egg yolk glaze to the pastry. Bake the chicken for 2 hours.

4- Part way through the cooking period, when the pastry becomes well browned, cover it with aluminum foil to keep it from burning.

5- When you are ready to serve, place the casserole directly on the dinner table and break the pastry seal with a large knife. Everyone will savor the mouthwatering, appetizing aroma. Spoon the cooking juices over the chicken. Cut it into serving pieces and serve with potato puree, the bacon slices and the creamy shallots and garlic cloves baked in their skins.

Serves 6
Preparation time : 40 minutes
Cooking time : 2 hours

1 whole Bresse chicken, weighing about 2 1/2 lbs., prepared by your butcher
6 slices of smoked bacon
10 large shallots
8 garlic cloves
1 roll of puff pastry
1 egg yolk for glazing
3 *bouquets garnis*
1 3/4 oz. olive oil
fleur de sel and freshly ground pepper

A longstanding tradition of poultry rearing between the Saône and Jura

The geographical location of Bresse largely explains this regional infatuation with chicken. An undulating plain runs across the borders of several departments from the Ain to Jura and across the Haute-Saône. There are a number of large cities here. In Lyon, Dijon, Chalons and even Geneva, people have long relished capons and chicken from Bresse. To respond to this demand, production became highly organized very early on. Women took responsibility for poultry rearing, while men tended to the fields or herds of cattle.

The entire region shows the mark of this extra source of wealth. Louhans, a little town in the well-tended countryside, has taken on the air of a lavish fortified city. Workshops and businesses stand along the main street under stone arcades carved in the Renaissance. The poultry fairs that have been held here since the Middle Ages are displays of the entire region's output of chicken, *poulardes* (adult chickens which have not yet laid eggs), and capons (castrated roosters). These birds will next be encountered on the finest tables in France.

The queen of poultry

The presence of large towns does not explain everything, however. The poultry of Bresse owes its current success to its high quality. Its reputation had deteriorated, but was reestablished in 1957 with the strict standards associated with an *Appelation d'origine contrôlée* (AOC), just like a great wine.

It all began with intense selectivity in defining the characteristics of the breed. Originally, there were gray, black and white chickens; only the white—with their national colors (blue feet, white plumage and red crests) passed the AOC test, emphasizes Georges Blanc. These

requirements are taken very seriously. Chickens are no longer bred on the farms, but are hatched in selection centers, which play the same role for chickens as stud farms do for horses. The early months of these chickens' lives are enviable. A *poulet de Bresse* must grow up free range in the open air, enjoying the acres of rich grass that surround the farms. Chickens are led out to pasture here just as sheep and cattle are elsewhere. They feed on seeds, grass and earthworms, which give their meat a distinctive flavor.

« With their breeders and their officers, their debates and their banquets, the local poultry fairs called « Glorieuses » have the feel of an agricultural show organized by the Third Republic. »

Then comes the time for force feeding. The breeders gather the chickens at night when they are drowsy. In the glow of electric light, they are put in wooden cages called « epinettes« , which will be their home for the next two weeks. Though they lose their freedom, they do get plenty of their favorite food— ground corn soaked in milk or whey. Corn is another of the region's riches, a treasure that used to be hung to dry by farmhouse doors as a symbol of prosperity. Local dairy cows are the chickens' neighbors in the pastures, and making *fromage blanc*, another regional treat, produces plenty of whey that is put to good use in chicken feed.

All this work results in rich, tender chicken that is cut up into eight pieces and roasted to seal in its juices. Cream is added to enhance the texture and blend with all the flavors of the meat. Everyone here embraces the extraordinary cult of this gourmet ritual.

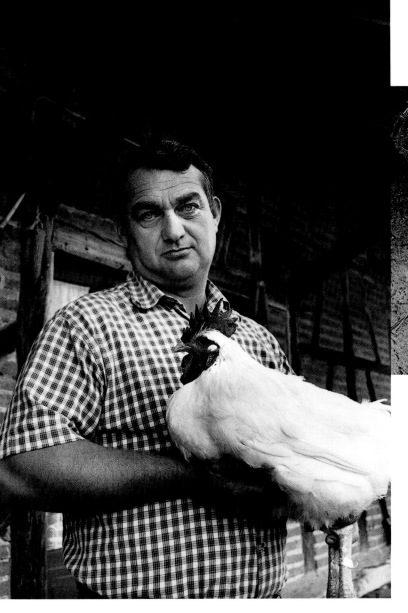

« Les Glorieuses »

Every year, local people throng to pay homage to these chickens with spectacular celebrations. The gatherings are appropriately named « Glorieuses », special fairs that are basically beauty pageants for chickens. In the third week of September, the festivities progress from Bourg-en-Bresse to Louhans to Montrevel and Pont-de-Vaux. « Nobody would miss it, » explains an agricultural worker who has spent his whole life working on the same farm. No one ever fools around when the great day arrives. In one corner of the farmhouse room, there are carefully framed diplomas and certificates, yellowed with age, honoring this breeder's poultry. It has been a long time since the vast tiled fireplace has been used, although it was impressive enough to get the farm classified as a historic monument. The speaker's voice is still full of respect as he recalls a golden age.

Every detail counts when it comes to winning at the « Glorieuses ». The chickens must be plucked with the greatest care, since any blemish on the silky smooth skin carries a penalty. They then have to be presented in a very particular way: the breeder folds the feet under the stomach and puts the chicken in two white linen cloths. The edges of the cloths are crossed under the stomach, then sewed together. The threads are criss-crossed, like corset lacings, and pulled together tightly to make an oval shape. Then the whole package is rinsed in cold water to shrink the cloth, compress the chicken and firm up the meat. The finishing touch is to tie a ribbon around the whole thing. With such a presentation, a chicken becomes a precious jewel, and it finds its home naturally, whether on the table of a smoky country bistro or under the frescoes of Paul Bocuse's establishment.

Above left
Raising chickens in Bresse used to be considered women's work, but men now share the activity equally. Shown here is Didier Grandjean, a breeder.

Above right
Returning from the market in Louhans.

Facing page
Before silos, the countryside's riches were displayed on houses all over the region of Bresse. Ears of corn were hung from roofs or stored in farmyard drying racks.

La poularde demi-deuil de la mère Brasier

Here is the recipe for one of Lyon's most celebrated specialties. The queen of chickens is prepared with a cream sauce seasoned with fresh truffles, commonly described as « in half mourning » for its black-and-white color combination.

Serves 6
Preparation time : 1 hour
Resting time : 48 hours
Cooking time : 1 hour 30 minutes

1 whole Bresse chicken, weighing about 4 1/2 lbs., prepared by your butcher
10 1/2 oz. smoked pork belly
5 1/2 oz. butter
5 1/4 oz. fresh truffles, washed and brushed
4 1/2 quarts chicken bouillon (You may use bouillon cubes.)
4 small carrots
3 turnips
2 celery stalks
4 leeks, white parts only
1 parsnip
salt and pepper

1- Cut the truffles into strips and slide them under the skin of the chicken over the breast and thighs. Truss the chicken and let it rest in the refrigerator for 48 hours so that the flavor of the truffles permeates the chicken.

2- The day you are cooking the chicken, peel and wash the vegetables and cut them into large pieces. Cook them in a large pot in half the butter for 15 minutes without allowing them to brown. Add the smoked pork cut up into large slivers, then add the bouillon and cook 10 minutes over low heat.

3- Season the bouillon with salt and pepper. Immerse the chicken in the simmering liquid for 1 hour. Turn off the heat and let it rest 20 minutes in the cooking liquid.

4- Drain the vegetables and place them on a large serving platter. Cover them with food wrap and keep warm. Remove the chicken from the bouillon. Set it aside and keep warm. Reduce the cooking liquid by half.

5- Remove the pot from the heat. Add the rest of the butter, cut into small pieces, and whisk vigorously to « inflate » the sauce. Correct the seasoning.

6- Place the chicken in the center of a serving platter. Surround it with the vegetables, cover it with the hot cream sauce, and serve.

You may also serve the chicken cut up into serving pieces, covered with the hot sauce, and accompanied by the vegetables.

La poularde pochée à la crème ou « sauce suprême »

Serves 6
Preparation time : 20 minutes
Cooking time : 1 hour 40 minutes

1 whole Bresse chicken, weighing about 2 1/4 lbs., prepared by your butcher
5 1/4 oz. butter
10 1/2 oz. thick *crème fraîche*
3 egg yolks
4 1/2 quarts chicken bouillon (You may use bouillon cubes.)
2 small carrots
2 turnips
2 celery stalks
2 leeks, white parts only
1 *bouquet garni*
2 onions, peeled
2 cloves
juice of 1 lemon
salt and pepper

1- Peel and wash the vegetables and cut them into large pieces. Cook them in a large pot with half the butter for 15 minutes without allowing them to brown.

2- Pour over the bouillon. Add the onions, stuck with the cloves, and the *bouquet garni*. Cook 10 minutes over low heat. Season with salt and pepper and immerse the chicken in the simmering bouillon for 1 hour. Remove from heat and let the chicken rest 20 minutes in the cooking liquid.

3- Carefully drain the vegetables and set them aside on a plate. Remove the onions and the *bouquet garni*, and cover the plate with food wrap to keep the vegetables warm.

4- When you are ready to serve, remove the chicken from the bouillon and keep warm. Reduce the liquid by half. Add the *crème fraîche* and cook another 10 minutes. Remove from the heat and add the egg yolks, the rest of the butter cut into small pieces, and the lemon juice, whisking the sauce vigorously to bind it. Correct the seasoning.

5- Place the chicken in the middle of a serving platter, cover it generously with the hot cream sauce, and arrange the vegetables around it.

Pissaladière in Nice

Whether it's called *pizza, pita, pompe,* or *fougasse,* bread dough stretched thin and baked in the oven is a rallying point for people all around the Mediterranean. *Pissaladière,* however, requires very specific ingredients: olive oil and olives from Nice, a compote of onions, and *pissalat,* if possible.

Above
An elegant pissaladière that still follows the rules at Dominique Le Stanc's current restaurant La Mérenda in the old part of Nice. He was formerly chef at the Négresco.

Facing page
The son of Thérèse, a fishmonger on the Cours Saleya, returns from fishing and moors his boat in Nice's Vieux Port. Anchovies and sardines, the base of pissalat, can only be caught when springtime comes.

At some point, every elected official and tourist in Nice makes his way to find a table at Theresa's place for a *pissaladière* or a piece of *socca,* another local specialty prepared with chickpea flower. Chirac and Jospin have been here, along with Alain Ducasse, a neighbor, who steps across the street to pay homage to his colleague.

Theresa's real name is actually not « Theresa »; it is Suzie. Before her time, there was Maria, whom everyone also called « Theresa.» The real Theresa lived in the 1920s; she used to set out with her portable stove and her baking racks to sell her *pissaladières* on the Promenade des Anglais. The business later settled down on the Cours Saleya in the heart of old Nice, and on market mornings, hot *pissaladières* would be delivered by moped hour after hour from a bakery on Rue Droite. Myths live on, and this legend has a life of its own. To follow in

Theresa's footsteps, you have to play her part and assume her name.

To each his own recipe
Pissaladière is the ultimate Niçoise specialty. However, there are not many people who start its preparation at five o'clock in the morning as Theresa does, patiently kneading the dough with olive oil, after simmering onions overnight on a woodburning stove and baking the dish in the oven until it takes on a beautiful golden color. Elsewhere, people will recommend a simple bread dough, a short pastry, or even puff pastry. They will tell you that a little honey counteracts the onions' acidity, that you should add some tomato as they do in the Breil valley. There is the question of anchovies, whether filets or pureed, or no anchovies at all, Menton style. Everyone in the region has his own secret, but no one seems to quite be able to compete with the dish the way it is prepared here in the lanes of old Nice.

For over fifty years, people in Nice have been eating *pissaladières* on wooden tables set up on Rue Renée-Socca, under the arbor at the restaurant El Jesu, in every bakery, or bought on the run from a kiosk.

Le pissalat

Pissalat is an indispensable condiment for the preparation of a good *pissaladière*. In Nice, it is also eaten with cold meats, hors d'oeuvres, and grilled fish.

1- Remove the heads from the fish and gut them. Arrange a layer of fish about 3/4-inch thick on the bottom of a terrine. Cover with a layer of salt, 1 clove, a few peppercorns, 1 bay leaf, and a few sprigs of thyme. Repeat these steps until you have used all the ingredients.

2- Set the terrine in a cool place and let it rest 1 week. Remove the layer of oil that rises to the surface and stir the fish mixture with a wooden spatula. Repeat this step (removing the layer of oil and mixing) once a day for the next 3 weeks.

3- At the end of this time, put the fish mixture through a sieve to remove the bones, the scales and the seasonings. Put the puree in a bowl and cover the surface with a thin layer of olive oil. Store the condiment in the refrigerator. (It will keep for about 3 months.)

A short-cut variation

Soak salted anchovies for 12 hours in fresh water, then put them through a sieve. Blend the resulting paste with 2 sprigs of thyme. Season with 2 cloves, cover with 1 3/4 oz. olive oil and store in a closed container in the refrigerator.

Makes enough for 5 or 6 *pissaladières*
Total preparation time : 1 month

2 lbs., 2 oz. sardines and anchovies
8 3/4 oz. sea salt
3 cloves
3 bay leaves
2 large sprigs of thyme
peppercorns
olive oil

La pissaladière

This is the recipe for the traditional *pissaladière* prepared by Dominique Le Stanc in his restaurant La Mérenda in Nice.

1- Salt the onions lightly and cook until soft for 1 hour in a covered frying pan over very low heat with the garlic, thyme, sugar, 1 1/2 oz. of the olive oil, and pepper until they are « melted.» The onions should be cooked but not browned.

2- Roll the bread dough out into a round 6-inches in diameter. Place the dough in a pie dish and let it rise 20 minutes in a warm place. During this time, preheat the oven to 390°.

3- Bake the dough 10 minutes to dry it out. Remove from the oven and spread a layer of *pissalat* on top, followed by a thick layer of onions. Arrange the olives on top (and the anchovies if you haven't used *pissalat*).

4- Drizzle the rest of the olive oil on top and bake the *pissaladière* 15 minutes. Remove it from the oven and let it rest a few minutes.

5- Season the *pissaladière* with pepper and serve it hot or at room temperature, with a white Saint-Joseph from Villars-sur-Var. The *pissaladière* will keep in a cool place for about 4 days.

Serves 6
Preparation time : 30 minutes
Resting time : 20 minutes
Cooking time : 1 hour 25 minutes

10 1/2 oz. bread dough
4 lbs, 4 oz. onions, peeled and finely minced
2 garlic cloves, peeled and crushed
3 oz. Nice olives
3 tablespoons of *pissalat* or 10 anchovy filets
1 sprig of thyme
2 1/2 oz. olive oil
pinch of granulated sugar
salt and pepper

Even Dominique Le Stanc, former chef at the Negresco, has tackled this specialty. In his chic bistro Mérenda on the Rue de la Terrasse, *pissaladière* or *tarte de Menton* is almost standard, displayed conspicuously on the counter at the beginning of the meal. Luscious and prepared with loving care, this dish does honor to the spirit of Nice.

Anchovies, onions and olives; an inseparable trio

You can relish the flavor of the entire Mediterranean world, as well as Nice, when you sample a *pissaladière*. Together with the olive oil of Provence, wheat has been the foremost staple here since antiquity, a vital ingredient during tough times as well as on festival days. F*ougasse* and *pizza Napolitaine* are equally dependent on this duo. After the day's work was done in bakeries, it was customary to roll out a little bread dough, season it with olive oil (butter and cream were not generally available) and top it with whatever was on hand. In Nice, these ingredients were onions, olives and anchovies, an elemental trio, but one that is also replete with its own subtleties.

The onions are quite straightforward; they come from local market gardens and are an ingredient common all over the Southeast. Anchovies, however, are a more complicated matter. At first, you would assume that they are the uncontested kings of Niçoise cuisine, the principal ingredient in the famous *anchoyade* that lends its inimitable flavor to salads. But does *pissaladière* call for ordinary anchovies? The etymology of the word *pissaladière* suggests otherwise. When you say the word, you are basically saying « *pissalat* », « *peis salat* », or salted fish.

> « *The anchovies are pretty much gone, and* pissalat, *which has to be made with special fish, is only produced in very small quantities now.* »

« You take salted anchovies and crush them with olive oil, » explains a merchant in old Nice who sells a version of *pissalat* year round. The traditional way is something else entirely, however. Real *pissalat* is made from the tiniest sardines and young anchovies too small to be sold; fishermen used to salt them for a few weeks and then put them through a sieve. Monsieur Desrumeaux, who makes *pissalat* and *rouille d'oursins*

the old-fashioned way in the Èze highlands, explains, « It's really a compote of fermented fish that they used to spread on the *pissaladière* between the dough and a layer of onion. » This type of *pissalat* scarcely exists these days, and is made only in minute quantities during anchovy fishing season. Purists concur; to make his *pissalat*, Desrumeaux has to buy his fish in Marseille.

The land of olive trees

The olive is more fortunate. It plays two roles in the traditional recipe: whole, added in the last moments of baking, and in the form of oil. In both cases, it's the « caillette », a small oval olive native only to this area, that makes this contribution. The Romans were partial to this type of Niçoise olive, but twenty years ago it had almost disappeared. Today, young growers are re-planting these olive trees on the terraces, and an AOC designation is being established for « caillettes.» Monsieur Piot presides over the eminent house of Almari in the heart of old Nice, and

> « Pissaladière *reminds me of Sundays in the country house, family picnics on the pebbles by the waves, snacks in the meadows and aperitifs with friends when you sit down at the table before you're really hungry.* »

sells his oil retail, directly from huge aluminum vats. His ancestors built their hydraulic mill in 1868 at the end of the Vallon de la Madeleine. Ever since, Alziari has continued to work the traditional way, using the excellent pressing method known as « à la genoise.» The olives are crushed in a stone press which is then filled with cold water, allowing the oil to be separated from the olive paste. Then all you have to do is decant it. The oil you get this way is intensely fragrant.

Few would use so rich a treasure as this oil in a *pissaladière*. But that is the strength of this simple dish: it holds it own even with oil of lower quality and anchovy filets standing in for *pissalat*.

La pissaladière de rougets d'Alain Llorca

Alain Llorca, who orchestrates the kitchens of the Hotel Négresco in Nice, has revisited the *pissaladière* for the delectation of his clientele. He makes the dish with a chickpea flour dough and little *rougets barbets* poached in olive oil.

Serves 6
Preparation time : 35 minutes
Resting time : 1 hour
Cooking time : 40 minutes

12 small filets of *rouget barbet*
5 1/4 oz. chickpea flour
3 1/2 oz. olive oil
5 sprigs of fresh basil
2 oz. *pissalat*
3 large onions
30 Nice olives
salt and freshly ground pepper
deep fryer with olive oil

1- Peel and mince the onions. Let them cook down over very low heat for 20 minutes in half the olive oil.
2- Meanwhile, mix the chickpea flour with 17 oz. water, whisking. Blend this mixture in a food processor and pass it through a fine sieve. Pour the batter into a large pot and let it thicken, stirring it constantly for 15 minutes as you would polenta.
3- Place the chickpea mixture in a large greased pastry tray and spread it into a smooth layer, about 2-inches thick, with a spatula. Refrigerate 1 hour for the dough to firm up.
4- Cut the chickpea dough into 6 rounds, each about 4-inches in diameter, with a cutter. Preheat the oil in the deep fryer to 360°. Fry the rounds two at a time in the deep fryer. When they are crusty and well browned, drain them on absorbent paper. Strip the basil leaves from their stems and fry the leaves.
5- When you are ready to serve, season the fish filets generously and poach them in the rest of the olive oil. Place each fried chickpea round on an individual plate, and spread the center of each with a thin layer of *pissalat* and then a thicker layer of « melted » onion.
6- Arrange the fish filets, just barely cooked through, on top of each round. Season with salt and pepper. Decorate the plates with the fried basil leaves and Nice olives. Season with freshly ground pepper and serve very hot.

Les tomates froides farcies de pissalat et fondue d'oignons

Pissalat may be used in various ways: in snacks, with grilled peppers, or in omelets. In this recipe it seasons a stuffing equally suitable for tomatoes and zucchini.

Serves 6
Preparation time : 20 minutes
Cooking time : 45 minutes

6 large tomatoes
6 onions
1 3/4 oz. olive oil
3 1/2 oz. *pissalat*
5 1/4 oz. Nice olives (or 3 1/2 oz. olive puree)
1 bunch of basil
2 garlic cloves
8 tablespoons sherry vinegar
2 tablespoons thyme leaves
salt and freshly ground pepper

1- Cut off the tops of the tomatoes and set aside these « hats.» Carefully remove the seeds and flesh from the tomatoes with a small spoon. Spread equal amounts of the *pissalat* on the bottom of each tomato.
2- Remove the pits from the olives and chop them. Peel and mince the onions and the garlic. Heat half the olive oil in a thick bottomed pot. Sauté the onions and garlic in the hot oil, turn down the heat, and cook over low heat for 25 minutes, stirring.
3- Midway through the cooking time, add the chopped olives (or olive puree) and the thyme leaves. Season with salt and pepper and stir. Fill the tomatoes with the onion mixture.
4- Arrange the tomatoes in an earthenware cooking dish. Replace the « hat » on each one, and drizzle them with the remaining olive oil. Bake them for 20 minutes at 320°.
5- When the tomatoes are done, arrange them on individual plates and let them cool to room temperature. Spoon up the cooking juices and whisk them together with the vinegar. Wash the basil leaves and cut them in half. Let them infuse in the vinegar-cooking juice mixture.
Serve the tomatoes warm or chilled, drizzled with the vinaigrette.

Fiadone in Corsica

Lemons ripen beside the houses in Corsica's tranquil coastal villages, but *brocciu* comes from high in the mountains. Made from whey by shepherds, this cheese is as mysterious as the mists on Mont Cinto. *Fiadone*, which combines both ingredients, embodies the spirit of the island for Corsicans themselves.

Above
Fiadone and preserved Corsican mandarin oranges at the farmstead inn Campu di monte in Murato.

Facing page
Marie-Paule Cesari prepares brocciu in Cap Corse.

Picture Cap Corse, with the sea far below; there is an unbroken view across the scrubland as it slopes steeply down to three cypresses by the cemetery in the distance. Most of the houses are closed and locked until the mainlanders return. But Anna Cecchi spends her winters in the village. For as long as she can remember, she has always made *fiadone* when her nephews come for vacation. On their first day, lunch invariably begins with *figatelli* and raw ham bought the week before from the traveling grocer's little truck; then she serves a *chapon* (here the word refers to a rock fish, a variety of *rascasse* that is baked with capers and tomato), which you can only get your hands on if you are a personal acquaintance of the fishermen. A nice strong cheese follows, and finally she presents all of Corsica in just one dish: *fiadone*.

During August, she does the best she can with the *brocciu* then available, a commonplace goat cheese. To get genuine *brocciu*, you have to come back in February or March, when the sheep have spring milk. In the summer, the goats no longer have their kids, so their milk dries up. That is a loss for people who are just passing through. They have only a sadly diminished taste of the island on their tongues as well as in their memories.

Eggs, *brocciu*, and lemon
Cookbooks written in Italian in the sixteenth century refer to this pastry. Travelers enjoyed it in the nineteenth century. These days, there is not a single Corsican bakery that does not sell it by the piece. Residents of the village of Corte claim to have invented the recipe, but they do not have any monopoly over it now. *Fiadone* is made on Sundays

« *This golden cake, which should contain no flour, is the very image of Corsica. It is like a distant dream.* »

Le fiadone

1- The day before you prepare the *fiadone*, hang the *brocciu* in a towel to drain over a large bowl to extract the maximum amount of liquid possible.

2- The next day, remove the zest from the lemons with a vegetable peeler. Chop the zest and cook it 5 minutes in boiling salted water.

3- Crack the eggs and separate the whites from the yolks in 2 large bowls. Beat the yolks with the sugar until well blended. Add the *brocciu* and the chopped lemon zest and mix again to combine well. Preheat the oven to 340°.

4- Butter a baking dish. Beat the whites into peaks, and fold them carefully into the yolk mixture. Pour the resulting mixture into the baking dish.

5- Bake 40 minutes. The *fiadone* is done when it rises slightly, takes on a nice golden color and cracks on top. Let the cake cool before removing it from the baking dish. Serve cold.

Serves 6
Preparation time : 35 minutes
Draining time : 12 hours
Cooking time : 45 minutes

1 lb. fresh *brocciu*
6 eggs
7 oz. granulated sugar
1 3/4 oz. butter
2 pesticide-free lemons
salt

Le Migliacci « Casanova »

This traditional cake made with fresh brocciu and lemon is cooked on a chestnut leaf. It bears the name of the pastry cook in the village of Corte.

1- The day before you prepare the cake, soak the chestnut leaves for 30 minutes in warm water.

2- The next day, prepare the leavening mixture. Dissolve the baker's yeast in warm water in a large bowl. Add the sugar and flour without mixing. Cover it with a cloth and let it rise 1 hour in a warm place, such as near a radiator.

3- Prepare the dough. Combine the flour and sugar in a bowl. Make a well with your fingertips and break in the eggs. Add the grated lemon zest to the middle of the mixture and pour in the milk little by little, stirring. Continue to blend, folding in the *brocciu* and then the leavening. Shape the dough into a ball, cover it with a cloth and let it rise 5 hours in a warm place.

4- Punch down the risen dough with your fingertips. Flour a workspace and roll out the dough 1/2-inch thick. Cut 12 rounds 2-inch in diameter and place each one on a chestnut leaf.

5- Let them rest 15 minutes. Preheat the oven to 360°. Cook the cakes for 20 minutes. The *migliacci* are done when they are brown and very smooth. Remove them carefully from the oven and let them cool before serving.

Serves 6
Preparation time : 30 minutes
Resting time : 6 hours 15 minutes
Cooking time : 20 minutes

For the leavening
3 1/2 oz. milk
1 3/4 oz. baker's yeast
pinch of granulated sugar
3 1/2 oz. flour

For the dough
2 lbs. flour
5 1/4 oz. granulated sugar
5 oz. milk
zest of 2 lemons
5 eggs
1 lb., 12 oz. fresh *brocciu*
12 dried chestnut leaves

and feast days in Bastia as well as Ajaccio, in the villages as well as the mountains.

In *fiadone* at least, the ancient schisms of Corsica are obliterated; on both sides of the mountains, from north to south, along the coastline and high in the remote backcountry, the entire island recognizes itself in this cake.

This sense of unity begins to seem precarious, however, when you consider the numerous variations in the dish from town to town. In Ajaccio, they roll out a short pastry as a base for the mixture, while in the north people are content to just pour the batter into a buttered, floured mold. *Fiadone* is sometimes confused with its close cousins: *imbrucciata*, a little tart that uses a small amount of flour for binding, and, in some villages, with *falcullela*, a cake made from *brocciu* that is cooked in chestnut leaves. The basic ingredients are always the same, however—eggs, *brocciu*, and some lemon zest to add flavor. There is eloquence in this simplicity.

The jewel of a harsh, rugged land

For a long time, goats and sheep were the only source of wealth in Corsica. A century ago, the most prosperous peasants owned several acres near the shore where they could shelter their flocks in winter, and even more importantly, mountain pastures where their animals could graze in the summer. Transhumance was the common denominator all across Corsica, and was practiced even on the Cap, a long tongue of land which is the harshest and most rugged backcountry imaginable.

This migratory system has slowly disappeared, and the flocks are now generally settled in one place. The native scrubgrass has crept up to the thresholds of old houses, the ancient terraced wheat fields are engulfed by wild arbutus, and kitchen gardens have been abandoned. But some sheep and goats remain in flocks that make unexpected appearances, wandering across twisting roads with no living soul in sight. Some people complain that these free ranging animals damage the low walls built by their ancestors, but the villagers' distrust of the backcountry nomads is nothing new. Shepherds know how appease the townspeople with gifts of *brocciu* or other cheeses brought down from their mysterious mountain retreats.

A mysterious alchemy

Corsican shepherds make dozens of different cheeses, including *niolo*, *calenzana*, and *tommes*, both fresh and aged. *Brocciu*, protected by an AOC designation since 1983, is made from the byproducts of the production of all the other cheeses. The milk may come from sheep or goats. A Filetta, a little cheese factory in northern Corsica, combines both kinds of milk in its semi-artisanal *brocciu*, which fortunately is available at most of the island's supermarkets, even in summer.

Brocciu has its origin in the milk that is set to curdle under pressure as part of the cheese making process. When the curds are pressed in a mold, whey is produced. In the shadow of the sheepfold, this cool liquid is poured into a tin-lined copper pot (a « pagholu »), and heated over a wood fire. Then some fresh milk is added (not more than 35%). Under the combined effects of the whey and the heat, the milk quickly solidifies into a fragile block. Just as the mixture comes to a boil, the block crumbles. The pieces are scooped up with a skimmer, layered into molds (which used to be made of plaited rushes), and drained for one or two days. This is genuine *brocciu*. It can be used to stuff sardines, fill *cannelloni*, lend its richness to an omelet fragrant with mint, and, of course, brown to perfection in a *fiadone*.

The shepherds who made these pastries for feast days in the solitude of their sheepfolds probably flavored them with a glassful of the *eau-de-vie* that accompanied their regular meals. This mode of preparation still has its adherents, but most people have adopted the tradition of adding lemon zest. This is not an insignificant detail. The Corsican lemon, which commercial records show has been growing here since the eighteenth century, has developed a thick, bright yellow skin to survive the winters here, which are harsher that those of Spain and North Africa. Even so, lemons thrive only along the coastline and in the lowest lying areas. Like its cousins, the citron and the bitter orange, the lemon reminds us of radiant Christmastides and gardens dreaming in the sun. Lemons come from the seaside and *brocciu* from the mountains; *fiadone* truly has everything required to symbolize Corsica itself.

Above
The Grimaldis' flock grazes in the hilly scrub land around Rogliano in Cap Corse.

Les clémentines soufflées au fiadone

This is a novel, imaginative way to present *fiadone*.

Serves 6
Preparation time : 30 minutes
Cooking time : 50 minutes

8 large Corsican clementines
7 oz fresh *brocciu*
1/3 oz. butter
2 eggs
3 oz. granulated sugar
1 ounce « Mandarine Imperiale » liqueur
salt

1- Cut the tops from 6 clementines. Remove the flesh from the inside with a small spoon and reserve the pulp and membranes.
Remove the zest from the 2 remaining clementines with a vegetable peeler. Chop the zest and cook it for 5 minutes in boiling salted water.
2- Break the eggs and place the yolks and whites in 2 separate mixing bowls. Beat the yolks with the sugar until well blended. Add the *brocciu* and the chopped zest and mix again. Preheat the oven to 340°.
3- Cook the flesh of the clementines with the butter and liqueur in a small pot for 5 minutes. Let it cool, then add it to the brocciu mixture. Beat the egg whites until they form peaks and fold them gently into the brocciu mixture.
4- Fill the clementines with this mixture and arrange them in a baking dish. Bake for 40 minutes. The filling is cooked when it puffs up slightly, takes on a lovely gold color and cracks on top. Let the clementines cool slightly before serving. They may be served hot or cold.

—

Corsica

La polenta de châtaigne

Serves 6
Preparation time : 10 minutes
Cooking time : 40 minutes

2 lbs. 3 oz. chestnut flour
2 *figatellu* (Corsican pork liver sausages), cut into large pieces
10 1/2 oz. fresh *brocciu*
1 3/4 oz. butter
salt and pepper

1- Bring 3 1/2 oz. of salted water to a boil in a pot. Add the chestnut flour and pepper, stirring constantly with a large wooden spatula.
2- Keep stirring the polenta on the stove for about 20 minutes, removing it from the heat occasionally. Be careful not to let it burn. The polenta is done when it forms a ball around the spatula.
3- Sprinkle a clean towel with chestnut flour and place the ball of polenta in the middle. Let it cool slightly. Meanwhile, sauté the figatellu for 20 minutes with the butter in a large pan.
4- Cut the polenta with a string into several even slices and serve immediately in deep bowls, topped with the sautéed *figatellu* and fresh *brocciu*.

Les sardines farcies au brocciu

Serves 6
Preparation time : 1 hour
Cooking time : 25 minutes

24 sardines of equal weight
7 oz chard, green part only
7 oz. fresh *brocciu*
several sprigs of Italian parsley
2 garlic cloves
1 3/4 oz. olive oil
1 egg
salt and pepper

1- Scale the sardines and remove their heads, pulling them carefully backward to remove the entrails with them. Remove the backbone. The filets should remain attached to each other in a butterfly shape. Wash the sardines under cold water and dry them on paper towels.
2- Wash the chard and immerse it in boiling salted water for 5 minutes. Drain the chard, refresh it under cool water, and squeeze it in a cloth to remove the maximum amount of water possible. Wash and strip the parsley leaves from their stems. Peel and chop the garlic cloves. Blend the chard, the garlic, and the parsley in a food processor. Combine the chard mixture with the *brocciu* in a large bowl. Add the egg and mix together. Season with salt and pepper.
3- Preheat the oven to 410°. Spread the stuffing inside the sardines with the skin on the outside. Roll the stuffed sardines up one by one and fasten each together with a wooden toothpick.
4- Arrange the sardines in a large earthenware baking dish. Drizzle them with olive oil. Season with salt and pepper. Bake 20 minutes. Take the sardines out of the oven. Carefully remove the toothpicks. Serve the sardines very hot, accompanied by a green salad with fresh herbs, such as basil or tarragon, and slices of toast rubbed with tomato and seasoned with olive oil.

Provence

Le bœuf en daube

Serves 6
Preparation time : 1 hour
Cooking time : about 3 hours

2 pieces of stewing beef, each weighing about 1 lb.
7 oz. barding bacon fat
3 1/2 oz. smoked bacon
1 1/2 liters red wine from Provence
2 tomatoes, cut into cubes
10 1/2 oz. pearl onions
4 garlic cloves, crushed in their skins
2 teaspoons tomato paste
5 oz. olive oil
1 oz butter
1 3/4 oz. flour
1 teaspoon granulated sugar
1 *bouquet garni*
1 tablespoon chopped parsley
1 pesticide free mandarin orange
regular salt, coarse salt, peppercorns and freshly ground pepper

1- Heat 3 1/2 oz. of the olive oil in a large cast iron pot. Tie the pieces of beef in barding fat and sauté them in the hot oil until they are browned. Lower the heat. Add the cubed tomatoes, the *bouquet garni* and the crushed garlic cloves in their skins. Cook a few minutes, then stir in the flour.
2- In a large bowl, mix the wine with the tomato paste. Pour into the pot. Add 8 1/2 oz. water, a small handful of coarse salt and a few peppercorns. Mix and boil together 5 minutes. Skim the broth. Lower the heat and simmer 3 hours.
3- Remove the zest from the mandarin orange with a vegetable peeler. Add it to the pot. Peel the onions. Caramelize them in a small pot with the butter, the sugar, and 8 1/2 oz. water. When they are nicely browned, set them aside on a plate.
4- Slice the smoked pork into wide strips. Sauté them with 1 3/4 oz. olive oil and combine with the onions. When the *daube* is thoroughly cooked and tender, add the onions and the pork with their cooking juices. Simmer several minutes more. Correct the seasonings, adding salt and pepper to taste. Sprinkle with the chopped parsley and serve very hot with gnocchi.

Les calissons d'Aix

Makes 20 *calissons*
Preparation time : 40 minutes
Cooking time : 6 minutes

For the dough
10 1/2 oz. ground almonds
10 1/2 oz. granulated sugar
3 tablespoons apricot jam
1 3/4 oz. candied orange rind, chopped
1 teaspoon vanilla extract
2 tablespoons cornstarch

For the glaze
1 egg white
3 1/2 oz. confectioners' sugar

1- First prepare the glaze. Combine the egg white and the sugar and whisk vigorously for 5 minutes until you have a whitish mixture. Cover with food wrap and set aside.
2- In a food processor, mix the granulated sugar, the ground almonds, the chopped orange rind, and the apricot jam. Add the vanilla and mix again until thoroughly blended.
3- Put the dough into a small pot and let it dry over low heat for 3 minutes, stirring constantly with a wooden spatula.

work surface. Roll out the *calisson* dough 3-inches thick. Allow it to cool. Preheat the oven to 340°.

5- Using a spatula, spread the glaze over the dough. Cut into wide strips with a large knife, then cut each strip into small lozenges. (Run the knife under hot water to facilitate the cutting.) Arrange the *calissons* on a pastry sheet covered with greaseproof paper. Bake the *calissons* for 3 minutes and let them cool on the pastry tray.

You may substitute pieces of preserved melon for the apricot jam, and use sheets of unleavened bread instead of the cornstarch as they do in Aix.

L'aïoli

Serves 6
Preparation time : 20 minutes
Soaking time : 24 hours
Cooking time : 1 hour 15 minutes

For the sauce
10 garlic cloves
1 egg yolk
3 1/2 oz. olive oil
salt and pepper

For the accompaniments
2 lbs., 2 oz. salt cod, left in one piece
4 carrots
3 leeks
4 turnips
8 potatoes
17 oz. fish stock (You may use powdered fish stock if available.)
coarse salt and pepper

1- The day before you prepare the *aïoli*, cover the salt cod with fresh water and soak for 24 hours, changing the water several times.

2- The next day, wash and peel the carrots, turnips and potatoes. Cut the leeks in half lengthwise and wash them under cold running water. Combine the vegetable in a stewpot. Pour over the fish stock and 17 oz. water. Add a small handful of coarse salt, season with pepper, and cook 45 minutes over low heat.

3- Meanwhile, prepare the *aïoli*. Peel the garlic cloves. Mash the garlic thoroughly in a mortar and add the egg yolk. Salt lightly, and add a moderate amount of pepper.

4- Blend in the oil one drop at a time, stirring with the pestle, as if making a mayonnaise. When the *aïoli* becomes creamy and thick, it is ready.

5- Immerse the entire piece of cod in the cooking liquid with the vegetables. Cook 30 minutes more, always over low heat. When you are ready to serve, drain the vegetables and the cod. Arrange them on a large platter and serve the *aïoli* separately, directly from the mortar.

Le tian provençal

Serves 6
Preparation time : 45 minutes
Cooking time : 40 minutes

6 small zucchini
6 tomatoes
3 garlic cloves
2 shallots
5 oz. olive oil
3 1/2 oz. grated cheese
1 small bunch of parsley
1 sprig of thyme
1 sprig of savory
2 bay leaves
salt and pepper

1- Wash the zucchini and the tomatoes. Cut them into rounds 2-inches thick. Peel and chop the shallots and garlic. Wash and chop the parsley. Preheat the oven to 410°.

2- Grease an earthenware cooking pan with half the olive oil. Arrange a layer of the zucchini rounds, overlapping them. Sprinkle with the shallots, garlic and parsley. Cover the zucchini with a layer of tomato slices and repeat these steps until you have used all these ingredients.

3- Slide the thyme, bay leaves and savory between the layers of tomato and zucchini. Season with salt and pepper, sprinkle with the cheese, drizzle with the remaining olive oil, and bake 40 minutes.

5- Serve the *tian* very hot from its baking dish. The *tian* is delicious with small goat cheeses melted onto slices of country-style bread.

Les petits farcis

Serves 8
Preparation time : 1 hour
Cooking time : 55 minutes

8 small tomatoes
8 small round zucchini
8 small onions
5 1/4 oz. sausage meat
3 1/2 oz. chicken liver
10 1/2 oz. cooked ham
2 shallots, peeled and chopped
2 garlic cloves, peeled
several sprigs of parsley
3 1/2 oz. stale bread
1 egg
5 oz. olive oil
1/2 cup milk
2 tablespoons dry breadcrumbs
salt and pepper

1- Wash the tomatoes and cut the tops off. Immerse the zucchini and onions for 3 minutes in a pot of boiling salted water. Drain them and refresh them under cold water. Hollow them out with the point of a knife. Chop the flesh you have removed from the zucchini and onions. Blend the vegetables with the ham, the chicken liver, the garlic and the parsley in a food processor.

2- Remove the flesh from the tomatoes with a small spoon. Discard the seeds and set aside the pulp. Season the inside of all the vegetables with salt and pepper. Break the bread into pieces and soften it in a bowl with the milk.

3- Sauté the shallots in half the olive oil for 5 minutes. Add the sausage meat. Let it brown a few minutes, stirring. Add the drained soaked bread, the vegetable mixture, the tomato pulp, and the egg. Season with salt and pepper and blend the stuffing ingredients thoroughly.

4- Fill the zucchini, the tomato and the onion shells with the stuffing mixture. Sprinkle with the dried breadcrumbs. Drizzle with the remaining olive oil and bake 45 minutes in a preheated 360° oven. Enjoy the *farcis* hot or chilled.

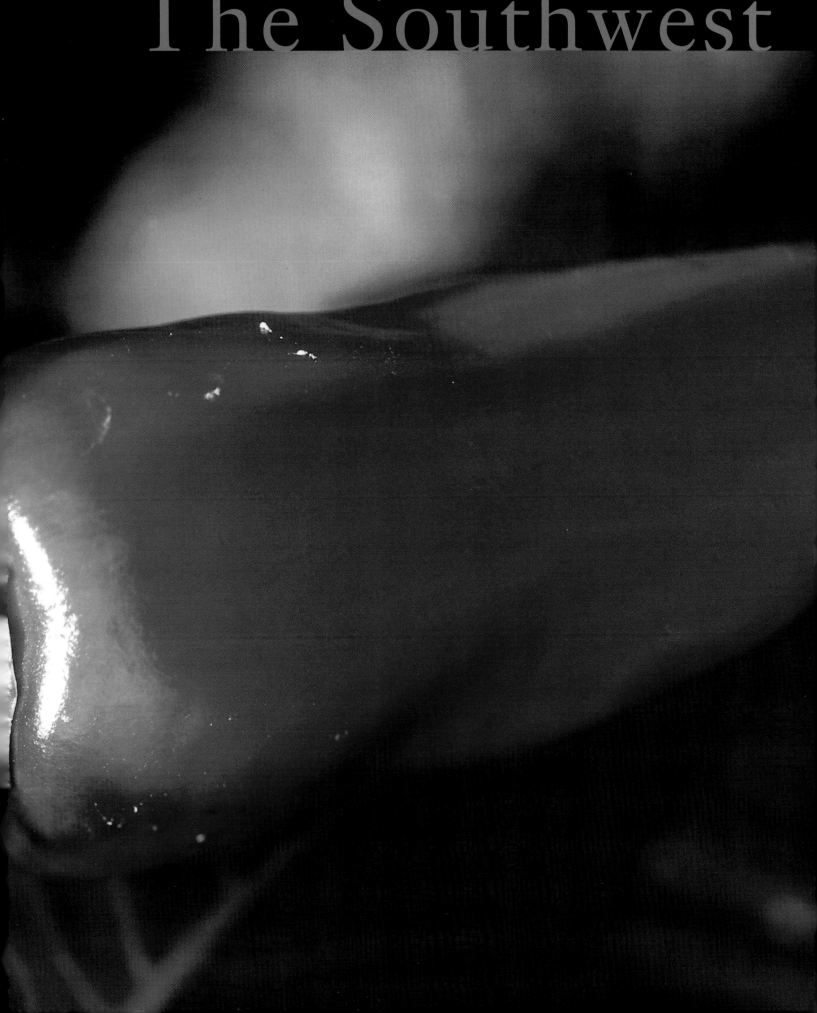

the southwest

Cassoulet at Castelnaudary

Castelnaudary considers itself the « world capital » of *cassoulet*, although when you speak with people there, they will admit that the situation is more complicated. There is actually a veritable trinity of *cassoulets* among Toulouse, Castelnaudary and Carcassonne. You might indeed say that the transfiguration of the bean, which renders this humble vegetable even more delicious that the meat that goes with it, approaches a miracle.

Above and facing page
The cassole, a cone shaped earthenware dish, is essential in making cassoulet, so that the beans can slowly absorb all the flavors of sausages and confit as they bake. Cooks will swear to you that the older the cassole, the better the cassoulet.

Prosper Montagné, founder of the *Larousse Gastronomique* wrote the epigram: « *Cassoulet* is the God of Occitane cuisine; God the Father is the *cassoulet* of Castelnaudary, God the Son comes from Carcassonne, and God the Holy Ghost emanates from Toulouse. » That says it all…almost. It is apparently true that the recipe, inspired by the *haricot de mouton* prepared by the Arabs with a base of fava beans and Indian peas, was established in Castelnaudary by the fourteenth century. The varieties of *cassoulet* far exceed Montagné's trinity, encompassing subtle variations in each village and even every household. Here, they might add a piece of mutton, there a partridge, a piece of aged bacon, a celery stalk, even a tomato. There are also debates over the type of bean: they use *tarbais* in the west, *pamiers* in Pamiers, *lingot* in Castelnaudary. « Chauriens » (as residents of Castelnaudary call themselves) have gone ahead and issued an official recipe, taking very seriously the role assigned to them in the creed promulgated by Montagné.

From rugby to *cassoulet*

Castelnaudary makes its living from *cassoulet*. Restaurants and *charcuteries* outbid each other for attention. In one restaurant, *cassoulet* is « royal »; in another, it is « imperial », « authentic », « traditional », or « old fashioned », but always and unfailingly, « *complet.* »
The Bouissou establishment, whose handsome sign is still the pride of the city, was the first to sell its *cassoulets* to tourists at the beginning of the nineteenth century. The great revolution dates from the 1970s, when five canneries set up shop near the city gates.

> « Even Castelnaudary's water tower looks like a giant « cassole », the word for the cone-shaped earthenware dish without which there's no cassoulet. »

The *confits de canard* may come from far away in Europe, and the beans often hail from Argentina, but that really does not matter. *Cassoulet*, formerly distributed in cans of uncertain origins, had finally found a homeland. Now *casssoulet de Castelnaudary* is actually made in Castelnaudary.
The oldest canning establishment is appropriately named La Belle Chaurienne, but the best known is owned by Laurent Spanghero, a farmer's son whose brother is the famous rugby star Walter Spanghero.

Le cassoulet

Beans for *cassoulet* are always prepared in exactly the same way; it is only the meat selection that varies from region to region. In Castelnaudary, they use a wide variety of pork (loin, ham, hocks, sausage, fresh rind), and also goose or duck *confit*. In Carcassonne, they add lamb, and sometimes partridge during hunting season. In Toulouse, the dish is prepared with pork belly, Toulouse sausage, mutton, and *confit*. This recipe given here is an adaptation of one of Prosper Montagné's.

Serves at least 10
Preparation time : 1 hour
Soaking time : 2 hours
Cooking time : 5 hours

For cooking the beans
2 lbs, 2 oz. white beans
10 1/2 oz. pork belly
7 oz. fresh pork rind
1 carrot, peeled
1 *bouquet garni*
1 onion
1 clove
3 garlic cloves, crushed

For the *cassoulet*
3 1/2 oz. goose fat
1 lb., 6 oz. pork shoulder
1 lb. lamb shoulder, boned
and cut into pieces
14 oz. garlic sausage
14 oz. Toulouse sausage
6 pieces of goose or duck *confit*
3 onions, peeled and chopped
1 *bouquet garni*
3 garlic cloves, crushed
5 tomatoes, seeded and cut into pieces
3 1/2 oz.. dry breadcrumbs
17 oz. bouillon from a *pot-au-feu*
(You may also use bouillon cubes.)
salt and pepper

1- Put the beans and the *bouquet garni* in cold water and soak 2 hours. Cook the beans in the soaking water with the *bouquet garni*, the crushed garlic cloves, the onion stuck with the clove, the carrot, the pork belly, and the rind over low heat

2- 40 minutes before the beans finish cooking, melt the goose fat in another pot. Sauté the pork shoulder and the lamb pieces. Season with salt and pepper and let the meat brown. Add the onion, the garlic cloves, and the tomatoes. Cover with the bouillon, add the *bouquet garni* and simmer for 30 minutes.

3- Remove the vegetables used to season the beans with 3 1/2 oz. of the cooking water, then add the pieces of pork and lamb together with their cooking juices. Add the garlic sausage, the pieces of *confit*, and the Toulouse sausage. Simmer gently for 1 hour.

4- Drain all the meat and set it aside on a platter. Slice the garlic sausages into thick slices and the Toulouse sausage into fine slices. Cut the lamb and pork into small, regular size pieces. Cut the pieces of *confit* in half. Set the pork aside on a plate.

5- Arrange the pork rind in a large glazed earthenware cooking dish (especially designed for a *cassoulet*) or a large oven-safe clay baking dish. Fill the baking dish with alternating layers of beans and meat, seasoning each layer lightly with pepper. Be sure the last layer consists of beans. Slice the pork belly and arrange on top. Moisten with a bit of the cooking juices. Sprinkle 10 1/2 oz. of the breadcrumbs on top and bake the *cassoulet* for 1 hour at 340°.

6- When a nice crust forms on top of the *cassoulet*, push it down with a spoon into the bean mixture. Sprinkle the remaining breadcrumbs on top and return the *cassoulet* to the oven for an additional hour. You may repeat this step several times.

A *cassoulet* is even better reheated. Prepare the dish the day before you intend to serve it. When you are ready to serve, add a little bit of bouillon to the baking dish, sprinkle it with breadcrumbs, and reheat in the oven for 40 minutes. When the crust is brown again, the *cassoulet* is ready to serve.

The Spanghero group not only has laboratory-like kitchens for preparing dishes and a fleet of trucks to distribute *cassoulets*, *magrets*, and other *confits;*
it also has its own slaughter houses, where just about all the pigs « d'Oc »that the region produces meet their fate. There was certainly plenty of expertise behind this success story, but also a celebrated name in Ovalie.

The affinity between *cassoulet* and rugby is evident every Sunday evening in Noé, about fifty kilometers from Toulouse. The owner of the restaurant Alex had the idea of treating visiting rugby teams to his version of *cassoulet*. The walls are a tapestry of rugby shirts worn by players from all over the world. As a television screen replays archived matches, dishes are set on the counter. No one here heeds the edicts emanating from Castelnaudary. This stew of *tarbais* beans is never browned in the oven; it has a fetching blush from the tomatoes that are added and could not care less about the title « *cassoulet*.» At the very most, it might lay claim to the name « *mongetada* », as it is called in the mountains of the Ardèche.

> « As Laurent Sanghero says in his distinctive accent, rumbling with 'r's', « Cassoulet *and* rugby get along very well together.» »

Her majesty the bean

Ignoring these local rivalries, the real strength of *cassoulet* is that, like the Canal du Midi, it links the gulfs of Gascony and Lyon and creates a sense of unity from the Pyrenees to the Corbières and the Massif Central. This is a dish with no pretensions, intended to be served to people at a common table. There was a time when *cassoulet* even added a little flavor to French politics. Armand Fallières, a native of Mézin in Lot-et-Garonne, insisted that his chef prepare *cassoulet* for him in the Élysée Palace when he became president. This was an era when debates in the Assemblée Nationale reverberated with the rugged accents of those Southwestern orators dubbed « *cassoulet* radicals » by their mean-spirited opponents. The story goes back to the beginning of the Republic. In 1848, the failing monarchy forbade political gatherings, but the left-leaning radicals of the Southwest did not engage in formal debates; they convened to eat. The tradition of the «republican

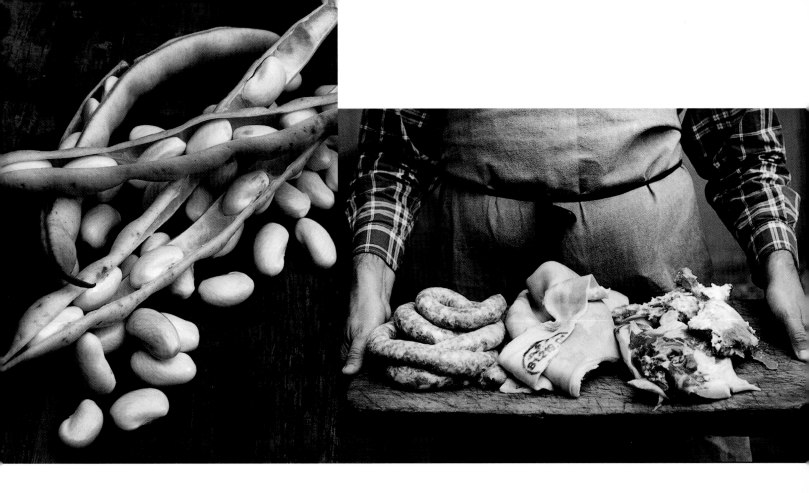

banquet», that combined good fare with lively rhetoric, was a natural evolution still alive today.

It is all one culture, but it is an open culture. As Vincent Pousson wrote in his book on the subject (*Cassoulets, haricots, mongets et Cie*): « The bean and its ancestors couldn't be tied down. *Cassoulet* is like the child of immigrants, long relegated to the outlying areas of our cuisine. In the end, our culture welcomed it because our sense of identity is strong. We digested and assimilated it, and *cassoulet* has become one of us; in fact, it has become our own heritage. » Chauriens hark back to the Middle Ages, but the *cassoulet* they boast of could not have existed before the sixteenth century when the bean, a native of South America, arrived in Europe. Legend has it that the legume bypassed France, in favor of Italy, and was only brought here by Catherine de Medici, wife of the future Henri II. In the foothills of the Pyrenees, the cultivation system for *tarbais* gives evidence of its exotic origins: growers make them climb up stalks of corn, their American compatriots. This method is inherited from the Native Americans, who also let their squash ramble over the soil in the same field.

A tradition reclaimed

What did people in Castelnaudary and its environs eat before the advent of beans? Probably a version of *cassoulet* made from fava beans, a vegetable cultivated in France since prehistoric times. This recipe is too good to be consigned to oblivion. We happily note that Dominique Toulousy, one the Toulouse's great chefs, has revived the dish in his restaurant on the Place du Capitole. Prepared with fresh fava beans, pork rind, and *confits*, this pre-Renaissance *cassoulet* is an incontrovertible delight.

About ten kilometers from Castelnaudary in the village of Labastide d'Anjou, Étienne makes his very own synthesis of all the *cassoulets* of the southwest. With sixty years experience, he remembers the time when *cassoulets* were carried to every village's bakery on Sunday to be cooked in their ovens. The baking dishes steeped in the fragrant smoke of the gorse and juniper that burned alongside them. Étienne has kept the essence of this heritage in his restaurant, which is a veritable museum of flavors. Earthenware *cassoles*, crafted by hand in a neighboring village, are made from the red clay of Issel. Time is the most precious ingredient of all. Seven hours of cooking, with three visits to the oven to break the crust. The transfiguration of the beans occurs ever so gently. The challenge is to make this humble ingredient end up « better than the meat » itself.

Facing page
Étienne Rousselot, undaunted at 70 years of age, has not abandoned his stove. Making cassoulet is a daily ritual in his inn in Labastide d'Anjou. Preparation time: seven hours, a magic number.

Above, right and left
Beans, Toulouse sausages, pork rind, confit: some of the ingredients for a cassoulet. Étienne (who also adds bacon and pork hocks) is firm on this point: « None of that makes a person fat. On the contrary, it helps burn cholesterol... »

Le cassoulet aux fèves de Dominique Toulousy

Serves 6
Preparation time : 1 hour
Cooking time : 4 hours

2 lbs., 2 oz. fava beans (You may use frozen fava beans.)
10 1/2 oz. Toulouse sausage
14 oz. pork shoulder, cut up into pieces
3 1/2 oz. goose fat
3 1/2 oz. pork rind
10 1/2 oz. garlic sausage
4 pieces of goose *confit*
2 onions, peeled and chopped
1 *bouquet garni*
3 garlic cloves, crushed
4 tomatoes, seeded and cut into pieces
3 1/2 oz. dry breadcrumbs
1 quart chicken bouillon (You may use bouillon cubes.)
salt and pepper

Before the introduction of haricot beans, *cassoulet* was prepared with fava beans. Dominique Toulousy, one of Toulouse's most admired chefs, has revived this recipe in his restaurant Les Jardins de l'Opera.

1- Immerse the fava beans in a pot of boiling water for 3 minutes. Drain them and refresh them under cold water. Remove their skins, and set them aside, keeping them cool.
Melt the goose fat in a large pot and sauté the pork shoulder in it. Season with salt and pepper and let it brown. Add the onions, the garlic and the tomatoes. Pour over the bouillon and simmer for 2 hours.
2- Add the garlic sausage, the *bouquet garni*, the pieces of *confit*, and the Toulouse sausage and simmer for another 30 minutes over low heat.
3- Preheat the oven to 340°. Drain the meat pieces and set aside on a platter. Cut the garlic sausage into large slices and the Toulouse sausage into thin slices. Cut the pork into small pieces and the pieces of *confit* in two. Arrange the pork rind on the bottom of a *cassoulet* dish. Fill the baking dish with alternating layers of fava beans and meat, seasoning with pepper. Make sure the last layer is consists of beans. Moisten with a little cooking liquid, sprinkle half the breadcrumbs on top, and bake for 1 hour.
4- When a nice crust forms on the top of the baking dish, push it back down into the fava bean mixture with a spoon. Sprinkle over the rest of the breadcrumbs. Put the *cassoulet* back into the oven for another 30 minutes. Serve very hot.

Le cassoulet léger de homard à l'estragon

Serves 6
Preparation time : 30 minutes
Soaking time : 2 hours
Cooking time : 2 hours 15 minutes

For cooking the beans
1 lb., 2 oz. white beans
1 *bouquet garni*
1 carrot, peeled
1 onion, stuck with a clove
2 garlic cloves, crushed and left whole

For cooking the lobster
2 large live Breton lobsters
3 sprigs of tarragon
17 oz. liquid *crème fraîche*
1 3/4 oz. lightly salted butter
1 teaspoon tomato puree
1 3/4 oz. peanut oil
1 3/4 oz. white wine
1 3/4 oz. dry breadcrumbs
salt and pepper

1- Soak the beans for 2 hours in cold water. Cook them 2 hours over low heat in the soaking water with the *bouquet garni*, the garlic cloves, the onion, and the carrot.
2- Meanwhile, immerse the lobsters in a pot of boiling water for 5 minutes. Drain them and remove the meat from the shells. With a small spoon, scoop out the « coral »(the creamy part) from the head of the lobsters and mix it with the butter. Set the flavored butter aside in the refrigerator.
3- Heat the oil in a large pot. Sauté the shells and heads and let them brown 5 minutes, crushing them with a spatula. Add the white wine and the tomato puree and stir. Moisten with 2 splashes of the cooking juices from the beans. Season with salt and pepper and reduce the lobster bouillon by half.
4- Strain the bouillon into another pot, pressing down hard on the shells to extract all their juices. Whisk in the *crème fraîche* and simmer 10 minutes. Preheat the oven to 340°.
5- Wash and chop the tarragon. Cut the lobster meat into slices. Drain the beans and put them into a large earthenware baking dish. Add the lobster slices and the chopped tarragon. Stir together and correct the seasonings.
6- Bring the lobster cream sauce to a boil and whisk in the coral-flavored butter. Pour the sauce over the bean and lobster mixture. Sprinkle with the breadcrumbs and bake the dish in the oven for 15 minutes at 360°. Serve the same day, lightly mashing the beans into the sauce to blend. (This *cassoulet* is not improved by reheating.)

Le cassoulet de morue

According to the members of the Brotherhood of the *Cassoulet*, the dish has always had a variation prepared with salt cod, with the fish taking the place of the *confit*.

1- The day before you prepare the dish, soak the salt cod for 10 hours, changing the water every 2 hours. (To save time, you may use a lightly salted cod filet and soak it just 2 hours.)

2- The next day, soak the beans for 2 hours in cold water. Cook them for 2 hours in the soaking liquid with the *bouquet garni*, half the pork rind, the garlic cloves, the onion, and the carrot. Cut the cod into 6 pieces. Preheat the oven to 340°.

3- Put the rest of the pork rind on the bottom and along the sides of a large ovenproof earthenware baking dish. Spread alternating layers of the beans and cod on top, seasoning each layer lightly with pepper. Make sure the last layer consists of beans. Cut up the smoked pork into slices and arrange them on top. Moisten with a little of the cooking juices. Sprinkle the breadcrumbs on top and bake 30 minutes.

When a nice crust forms on top, the *cassoulet* is ready to serve.

Serves 6
Preparation time : 30 minutes
Soaking time : 12 hours
Cooking time : 2 hours 30 minutes

For cooking the beans
2 lbs. white beans
7 oz. pork rind
1 *bouquet garni*
1 carrot, peeled
1 onion, stuck with 1 clove
2 garlic cloves, crushed and left whole

For cooking the salt cod
2 lbs., 2 oz. salt cod
7 oz. smoked pork belly
7 oz. pork rind
3/4 oz. dry breadcrumbs
pepper

Confit in Gers

Foie gras is the coin of the realm here, and it has always been exported to distant wealthy tables. But what to do with the goose and duck carcasses that remain? Every farmhouse has learned how to preserve these leftovers, which are far too valuable to be wasted. Legs and wings are salted before being cooked in their own fat. The popularity of the cuisine of the southwest accomplished the rest.

Facing page, above
Pampered, sheltered, and fed on boiled corn meal, ducklings flourish on every farm in the Southwest.

Facing page, below
In Monteils, Jacky Carles fought hard for permission to continue to cook his confits in copper pots. Approval was granted, thanks to professors at the University of Toulouse, who testified to help him obtain a special authorization from the European Commission. Copper is beneficial in very low doses.

A goose and three ducks are folded up into a shopping bag or tucked beneath an arm, their heads are hooded and hang down like so many trophies. A crowd throngs around the scales under the neon lights of the recently refurbished market. It is close to the end of the year, the big season for the *marché au gras* in Samatan. This event is the holy of holies for devotees of *confits*, *foie gras*, and other such delicacies. Sixteen tons of carcasses and one and a half tons of *foie gras* may be sold in a single session. In the days leading up to Christmas, as many as fifty tons of poultry can move in less than an hour.

Market day at Samatan
The ritual never alters. This trade is a very serious business, regulated, intense, and operating on a strict timetable. The vendors, mostly small scale local producers, arrive at 7:00 AM; they have two hours to set out their poultry, already gutted and plucked, on their stands. There are no embellishments and no prices are posted; the connoisseurs know their

way around. At exactly 9:30, the doors open and bargaining begins.

Some buy at the very last moment, some race in and out, others haggle. There are restaurant owners and poultry dealers, but most buyers are simply good cooks who are ready to spend their afternoons over their stoves. People come from Toulouse, Auch, and Montauban, and all over the Southwest. They rally to the region's traditions, its geese, ducks, and « bastides », those fortified towns built in a neat grid pattern around their real houses of worship, their marketplaces.

> « There are poultry markets every day in Gers, but they say Samatan is still one of the liveliest town squares in the whole Southwest on Mondays. »

They treasure savory memories of the days when their parents made *confits* in their farmyards. Although they are city dwellers now, they still treat themselves to these old fashioned, delectably slow-simmered dishes. *Confits* were worthy rivals of grandmothers' homemade preserves. Sterile canning methods have taken the place of copper cauldrons and earthenware pots, but these changes do not stand in their way. The happy recollections of a Sunday in the country simmers on the stove along with dinner

Le confit de canard

Serves 6
Preparation time : 10 minutes
Salting time : 24 hours
Cooking time : 5 hours

6 duck legs
1 garlic clove
7 oz. sea salt
3 lbs., 3 oz. duck fat (You may substitute goose fat.)
3/4 oz. peppercorns

1- The day before you prepare the dish, crush the peppercorns, and mix them with the salt. Arrange the duck legs in a large dish and cover them with the pepper and salt mixture. Cover them tightly with food wrap and refrigerate for 24 hours.

2- Remove the duck legs from the salt and wipe with a cloth. Melt the fat in a large frying pan. Immerse the duck legs in the hot fat and cook for 5 hours over low heat without stirring. During this time, watch to make sure the fat just simmers without breaking into a full boil.

3- When the legs are thoroughly cooked and tender, drain them and place them in a large bowl. If you wish to keep them for a long time (up to 3 months), cover them with the cooking fat and store in the refrigerator.

4- When you are ready to serve, reheat the duck legs in a skillet with a whole garlic clove, crushed in its skin, browning them lightly.

Serve the *confit* de canard nicely browned and crusty, with a side dish of potatoes and *cepes* sautéed together.

after a day in Samatan.

« It's very simple to make excellent *confit* for very little money if you have good ingredients, » assert a pair of teachers from the outskirts of Toulouse. They come every month to stock up. « You salt the pieces overnight and all you have to do the next day is cook them in their own fat. Once it's done, you can reheat it faster than you can sauté a steak. It's even less expensive. » A *confit* really is a bargain, since nothing goes to waste. The breasts go into the freezer to be cooked on the grill. The wings and drumsticks also get simmered in the fat, to be used in everyday cooking.

Ancient rituals

At 10:30, there is a fresh burst of activity: the *foie gras* market has just opened. In the Southwest, *confits* and *foie gras* are inseparable. You might routinely eat both in the course of one meal; people are not obsessed about diets in these parts. One course follows logically from the other. A *confit* worthy of its name can only come from a force-fed duck or goose. This practice is a requirement if the meat is to be rich and tender, falling off the bone at the touch of a fork; its juices mingle with its soulmates, potatoes *sarladais* or *landais* cooked with parsley and garlic (from Lautrec, of course). Magnificent *cèpes*, oddly called « from Bordeaux » instead of

« Gers » or « Perigord », go into the mix when they are in season.

The whole story began with the irresistible craving of the rich and powerful for *foie gras*. To satisfy this appetite, wealthy Romans would have entire flocks of geese herded to the capital from Gaul. Following a practice originated by the Egyptians and perfected in Rome, they would force-feed the ducks and geese to enlarge their livers and make the meat more flavorful. It seems that the Romans used grain and figs in this process, an idea that has recently inspired a small group of producers in Gers. They have begun raising ducks on a diet of nothing but figs, calling them « *Figuigers* » appropriately enough. What a treat!

« *When I was growing up,* foie gras *was what really mattered. Things have really changed since then.* »

Force-feeding was a common practice in Gers and elsewhere in Europe during the Middle Ages. Alsace made *foie gras* a local specialty as Hansi's engravings bear witness, and this Northeastern region established a longstanding monopoly in supplying the great courts of Europe with the delicacy. While others were preening, however, Gascony was hard at work, although in relative obscurity. One factor was corn, which made the voyage from the Americas in the holds of Columbus's ships; it revolutionized the country's agricultural, economic, and food industries from the eighteenth century on. The corn's color is of the utmost importance here; the kernels must be white to produce a pale yellow liver. Specific breeds had to be perfected for force-feeding–gray geese,

Pôt à
confit de
Castelnaudary
170,00F

Barbary ducks and special hybrids, coming from local stock and selected for their capacity to undergo the process.

The final component is the peasant common sense that dictates nothing be wasted. This thrifty impulse explains the widespread preparation of *confit*, another of those preserved foods so useful during lean times. Several times a month, in her « laboratory » at the end of a little road that rambles over corn-covered hillocks, Denise Bégué puts up her *confits* in old fashioned bowls in accordance with tradition.

Every morning, ducks and geese head out in flocks to the meadows, just like sheep. When it is time to begin the *gavage* (force-feeding), she reverts to an age-old technique: the very pale yellow corn is injected with a special funnel. « Force-feeding is absolutely an art. My husband takes care of the ducks, and I handle the geese. You find more force-fed ducks these days than geese, and that's because the feeding technique for geese is more difficult. You have to be close to the bird and treat it gently. Geese don't flourish in an industrialized setting. »

The taste of life

Herein lies the problem. Since *foie gras* and *confit* have become identified as pinnacles of French gastronomy, demand for them has increased steadily. In Gimont, which lies in the heart of Gascony, the Comtesse de Barry factory attempts to reconcile tradition with semi-industrialized production and vacuum-packing techniques. Founded in 1908, the company was one of the first to distribute its products throughout France, via fairs, exhibitions, and mail order. In 1940, Comtesse de Barry used a poignant theme in its advertising: a young woman daydreaming about her husband, a soldier at the front. « He might return at any moment. Always have a delicious French *conserve* on hand for him. » It was a recipe for success; just a few years later, the company Ducs de Gascogne set up shop a few yards away from the original Comtesse.

Then there are characters like André Daguin, a friend of politicians of all stripes, who labors over *magrets* and the full range of duck and goose cookery in his Hotel de France in Auch. There are television shows that have based their business on the cuisine of the Three Musketeers country. There are distributors determined to line up *foie gras* and *confits* on pre-holiday store shelves at any price. There are doctors who will assure you that goose fat is cholesterol-free, a healthful component of the « French paradox.» This trend has inspired a soufflé confection of movie-making, *Le bonheur est dans le pré* (« Happiness is in the Meadow »), a film directed by Étienne Chattiliez, which was shot in Vic-Fezensac, and changed forever the lives of the people of Gers. « After that movie was released, the phone never stopped ringing, » recalls Denise. « We couldn't satisfy the demand out there. » *Foie gras* and *confit*, thus promoted the entire region and its cooking into symbols of a rosy-cheeked tranquil France, savoring life itself with every mouthful.

Le foie gras des Landes confit aux épices douces d'Hélène Darroze

Serves 6
Preparation time : 40 minutes
Refrigeration time : 24 hours
Cooking time : 40 minutes
Resting time : 3 weeks

1 lobe of foie gras, weighing 1 lb., 5 oz.
2 lbs., 2 oz. duck fat
1/4 oz. powdered cloves
1/4 oz. powdered mace
fine salt
a spice blend consisting of 1/3 oz.
powdered cardamon, 1/3 oz. powdered
galangal, 1/4 oz. ground cinnamon, and
1/3 oz. ground Szechuan peppercorns

For the chutney
1 mango
1 pineapple
2 bananas
1 lime
2 garlic cloves
1/3 oz. rice vinegar
1/2 oz. fresh ginger
5 1/2 oz. brown sugar

Foie gras may also be prepared as a *confit* and preserved in its own fat, as Hélène Darroze offers it in her eponomously named restaurant in Paris's 7th arrondissement. In this recipe, the *foie gras* becomes even more creamy and flavorful.

1- Remove the membranes from the *foie gras*. Measure out 1/4 oz. of the salt and 1/4 oz. of the spice blend. Season the *foie gras* inside and out with the salt and spices. Wrap it in food wrap and refrigerate for 24 hours.
2- The next day, heat the duck fat in a large pot. When the temperature reaches 175°, immerse the liver in the hot fat for 10 minutes. Be very careful not to let the fat boil. Turn the *foie gras* carefully and cook 10 minutes more.
3- Drain the *foie gras* on a rack, being careful to preserve its shape. Refrigerate for 2 hours. Wrap it in food wrap, place it in a terrine and pour the cooking fat over. Refrigerate for 3 weeks.
4- A week before serving the *foie gras*, cut up the mango, the pineapple, and the bananas into small even pieces. Chop the ginger, the lime zest, and pulp. Bring the rice vinegar to a boil and add the fruits, lemon, ginger, brown sugar, and garlic cloves. Cook together for 15 minutes over high heat. Store the chutney in a bowl in the refrigerator.
5- The day you intend to serve the dish, remove the *foie gras* from the fat and take off the food wrap. Cut the *foie gras* into short, thick pieces and serve with the chutney and toasted slices of country style bread.

Le confit de poires au miel

Serves 6
Preparation time : 30 minutes
Cooking time : 45 minutes

3 pears
7 oz. liquid honey
3 vanilla beans
12 1/4 oz. sugar cubes

Fruits, vegetables, and flavorings may all be preserved in this sugar and honey syrup.

1- Peel the pears and cut them in half, being careful to keep a part of the stem attached to each pear half. Remove the cores and rinse the pear halves under cold water. Bring 17 oz. water and the sugar lumps to a boil. Immerse the pears carefully in the syrup, lower the heat, and cook 20 minutes over low heat. Preheat the oven to 320°.
2- Split the vanilla beans lengthwise and scrape the seeds out. Heat the honey in a small pot, add the vanilla seeds, and stir 1 minute before turning off the heat.
3- Carefully drain the pears and place them on a large earthenware platter. Pour the vanilla scented honey over them and bake 15 minutes, basting the pears with the honey syrup as they cook. Remove them from the oven and let them stand a few minutes. Serve the pears while still warm with a scoop of vanilla ice cream, and pour the honey syrup on top.

the southwest

Poule au pot in Béarn

When Henri IV promised all his subjects a chicken in the pot every Sunday, he made the dish a national symbol, while at the same time associating it with his own native land. Since then, *poule au pot* hails from Béarn, just as he did. This is certainly the way chefs in Pau view the matter. With rice or without, accompanied by a white sauce or tomato *coulis*, *poule au pot* is a feast for important occasions.

Facing page
Two fine hens, nice and plump and substantial enough to stand up to several hours of slow cooking.

Georges Lacrampe, one of the last independent poultry dealers in Béarn, is on the road all week long. The valleys of Aspe and Ossau hold no secrets for him. He goes from farm to farm and village to village, a peddler in quest of a nice fat chicken that has spent its life scratching in the farmyard, along country paths, and around manure heaps. He is on a quest for good egg layers past their prime, fowl two or three years old just ready for the stewpot. The real challenge in Béarn is to find a chicken worthy of going into a pot. A young chicken that has just achieved its full growth will not do; he needs a real full-grown bird, sufficiently firm-fleshed to stand up to three or four hours of cooking, ending up meltingly tender, but still presentable on a platter.

From yesterday to today...

This legendary dish is reserved for the most patient of cooks. Are its proponents so numerous that there is a shortage of the principal ingredient? The situation today is a far cry from the glory days of Georges Lacrampe's father, who was in the same business. « When I was growing up, there were chickens everywhere in the farms. The Sussex breed, all white with a few black stripes, the « faverolles », and the « viandottes », birds with very yellow meat. They were transported alive in cages. It was tough work. » These days, the demand has indeed abated. Most of the buyers are restaurants and farmhouse inns that continue to prepare this traditional dish when the first chills of winter set in. However, since the « poulaillers », those splendid wooden chicken coops that used to be suspended from balconies to defeat the foxes, are frequently unoccupied these days, the market is still tight.

« It was a tough profession. Buyers wanted to see the chickens alive, and they called the shots. It wasn't unusual for us to have to pluck them on the spot to get someone to buy them. »

« I only make *poule au pot* when it's ordered in advance, but in winter I have groups who come every week from all over the area, » relates Maryse Biscar in her farmhouse inn in Arbus, not far from Pau. It's a dish from their past. For many older people, it brings back the tastes of their youth. « *Poule au pot* should be savored in the appropriate setting, in houses with their old-fashioned sliding doors, with a

La poule au pot

This it the classic recipe for *poule au pot* as prepared by Bernard Coudouy de Laruns in the Pyrénées-Atlantiques, where a *poule au pot* festival convenes each autumn.

Serves 6
Preparation time : 45 minutes
Cooking time : 3 to 4 hours depending on the age of the chicken

1 chicken
3 carrots
2 turnips
1 leek
1 *bouquet garni*
3 1/4 quarts chicken bouillon (You may use bouillon cubes.)
salt and pepper

For the stuffing
giblets from the chicken
3 chicken livers
1 heel of country ham
10 1/2 oz. sausage meat
3 slices of bread
3 1/2 oz. milk
2 eggs
1 shallot
2 garlic cloves, peeled
1 sprig of thyme
1 bay leaf
2 sprigs of parsley

For the rice pilaf
14 oz. white rice
1 onion

For the white sauce
1 3/4 oz. butter
1 3/4 oz. flour
2 egg yolks
pinch ground paprika
24 oz. chicken bouillon

For the tomato sauce
4 tomatoes
3 shallots
2 green peppers
2 garlic cloves
1 3/4 oz. olive oil

1- First prepare the stuffing. Put the bread in the milk to soak. Chop the gizzards and the livers together with the ham, shallots, and garlic in a food processor. Squeeze out the excess liquid from the bread. Add the eggs and softened bread. Season with salt and pepper and blend all together to combine thoroughly.

2- Mix this stuffing with the sausage meat. Place the thyme, bay leaf, and parsley inside the chicken. Add the stuffing and sew the cavity closed with linen thread.

3-. In a soup pot, immerse the chicken in the bouillon, and add the *bouquet garni*, the pepper, and the salt and cook 3 hours over low heat. Drain and wash the turnips, the leek, and the carrots. Add them to the bouillon 1 hour before the end of the chicken's cooking time. When the chicken is done, turn off the heat and let it rest in the bouillon.

4- Prepare the rice. Skim the fat from the top of the bouillon with a small ladle. Heat the fat for 3 minutes in a pot together with the chopped onion. Add the rice and stir to coat each grain. Cook for 20 minutes, adding bouillon as necessary as the rice cooks. Season with salt and pepper.

5- Prepare the tomato sauce while the chicken is cooking. Cut all the ingredients into small pieces. Sauté them in the olive oil. Season with salt and pepper and let them cook down over low heat for 2 hours.

6- Prepare the white sauce just before serving. Melt the butter, add the flour, and blend with a spatula. Turn off the heat and pour over the chicken bouillon. Reheat while whisking. When the sauce begins to thicken, season it with salt and pepper. Remove it from the heat. Add the eggs and paprika, whisking vigorously to blend.

7- Serve the chicken cut into pieces, accompanied by the stuffing, the rice, and the vegetables on a large platter. Serve the two sauces alongside.

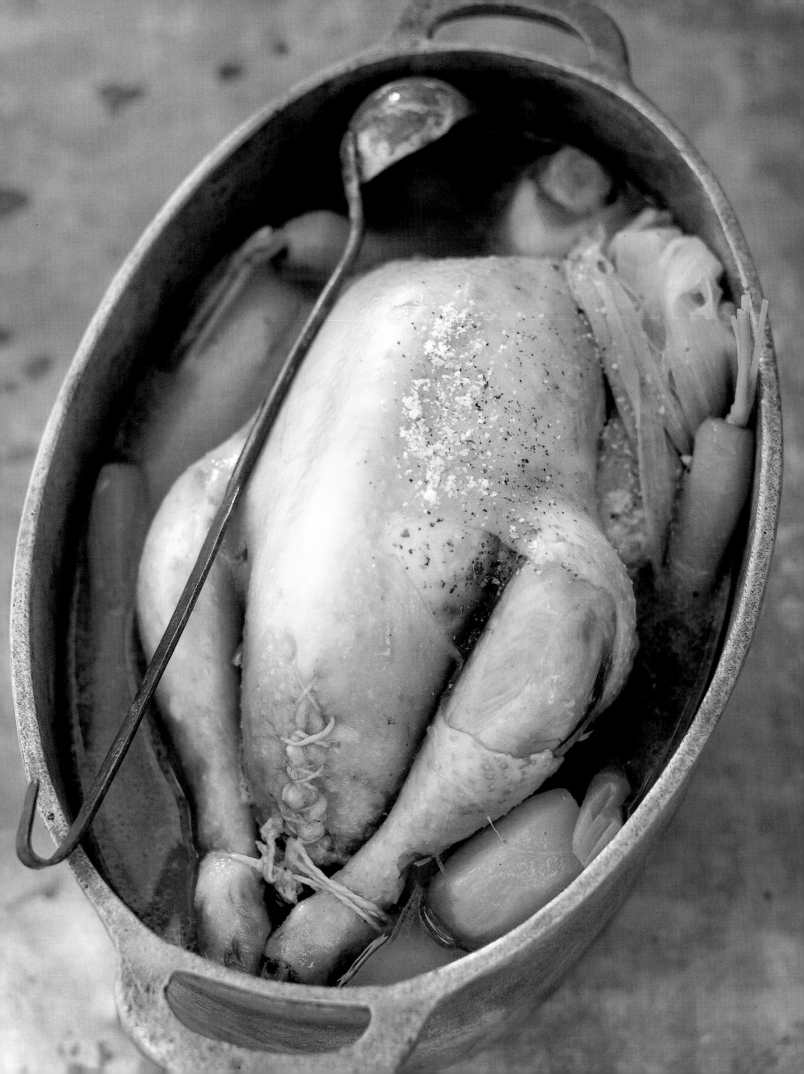

square courtyard glimpsed through an elegant wrought iron grill, draped with wisteria, and a palm tree reminiscent of the charms of the ocean.

...a dish that brings back memories

Is *poule au pot* really typically Béarnaise? We cannot be sure. The idea of putting superannuated birds into a stewpot is universal. This is just one more version of *poule au pot*, using the ingredients readily on hand. There are *poules au pot* in Gascony, the Vendée, and even Paris. One of the oldest restaurants in les Halles called the Poule au Pot. Even the sophisticated cuisine of Escoffier and Pellaprat embraced this thoroughly national dish in the strictly codified form of *poularde au riz sauce suprême*.

But *poule au pot* is truly distinctive in Béarn. Most importantly, for 400 years the Béarnais have had an ample supply of corn, the ideal feed for poultry, which gives the chickens' meat a golden color. We are not talking here about hybrid corn, which only became widely distributed in the 1960s; what people use here is the genuine article that the conquistadors brought back from America in the holds of their caravels. Every self-respecting farm in the region is flanked by a trellised corn dryer, a promise of feasts to come, even in winter.

Finally, we cannot forget Henri IV. The king was born in Pau and his castle stands here at the end of the Promenade des Pyrénées; he is still a local hero. When he succeeded to the French throne, Henri IV endowed the *poule au pot* of his childhood with a national destiny, as recorded by Hardouin de Péréfixe, bishop of Rodez, in a book published in 1664: « If God grants me life, I will see to it that there will not be a single laborer in my kingdom who cannot afford to have a chicken in his pot. »

Poule au pot and its variations

Old-timers in Béarn remember this Sunday treat as a Saturday custom. Younger chickens, considered more elegant, have largely replaced hens, which are considered too rustic for festive tables. But more recently the hens have had their revenge. The complex, time-consuming nature of their preparation has elevated their status, and hens are now considerably more expensive by the pound than younger birds.

Every household has its own recipe; in addition to the seasonal vegetables—carrots, potatoes, or turnips—there are countless variations. Some make stuffed cabbage for the occasion, some flavor the broth with pieces of *ventreche* (smoked peppered pork), others add tapioca, vermicelli, or *perles de Japon*. There are those who opt for rice, arguing that this grain was made popular by Henri IV and Sully; when cooked to pearly opacity in chicken fat and simmered in chicken broth with little onions, there is nothing better.

The sauces that go with the chicken are also a topic of heated debate. Some advocate a simple tomato *coulis* seasoned with a splash of oil. Others endorse a vinaigrette or swear by a light white sauce. The most enlightened are open to all three. Bernard Coudony, whose restaurant Arrégalet is in Laruns, is a fervent supporter of *poule au pot*. He stuffs it with mountain ham made by his brother and sews it up with a thick black needle bequeathed to him by his grandmother. He fought for years to have the Laruns cheese fair changed into a *poule au pot* celebration; this event is now held on the first weekend of October. For the love of his favorite dish, he has accepted an honor conferred by his neighbors, the Gascons; he has been anointed a *coq-chevalier* in the Order of the Stuffed Chicken by a brotherhood that holds its meetings in Moissac in the Tarn-et-Garonne department.

La terrine du pot, infusée à l'estragon

Serves 8
Preparation time : 30 minutes
Cooking time : 3 hours 45 minutes
Refrigeration time : 12 hours

1 Bresse chicken, weighing about
4 lbs., 4 oz., prepared by your butcher
4 carrots
4 turnips
2 leeks, white parts only
1 *bouquet garni*
1 onion
1 clove
1 bunch of tarragon
3 1/4 quarts chicken bouillon (You may use bouillon cubes.)
1 packet of Madeira gelatin mix
coarse salt, regular salt, and freshly ground pepper

This recipe can also make good use of leftover stewed chicken or other meat. The terrine should be prepared the day before you plan to serve it.

1- Immerse the chicken in a pot of boiling water for 1 minute. Drain and refresh under cold water.

2- Peel the carrots and the turnips and cut into large pieces. Split the leeks in half lengthwise and, rinse under cold water. Cut the leeks into strips.

3- Combine the chicken, the onion stuck with the clove, and the *bouquet garni* in a pot. Add a handful of coarse salt, pour over the chicken bouillon, and simmer 3 1/2 hours over low heat.

4- 1 hour before the end of the cooking time, add the vegetables. When cooked, drain and remove the chicken and vegetables, and reduce the bouillon by half. Turn off the heat and immerse the entire bunch of tarragon in the liquid to infuse for 20 minutes Meanwhile, remove the chicken meat from the bones.

5- Measure 1 1/2 quarts of the cooking liquid into a pot. Stir the tarragon around in the bouillon, then strain. Add the gelatin, whisking to dissolve. Correct the seasonings.

6- To facilitate unmolding the terrine later, cover the bottom of a porcelain mold with food wrap. Pour over a thin layer of the gelatin mixture. Arrange some of the vegetables and pieces of the chicken on top. Add another layer of the gelatin mixture and repeat these steps until the ingredients have all been used.
Refrigerate the terrine overnight.

7- Unmold the terrine and slice it with an electric knife. Serve with a walnut oil vinaigrette.

Variation

You may also use the breasts of farm raised chicken in this recipe. Cook the chicken breasts with the vegetables for about 45 minutes. Cut them up into small pieces and proceed with the preparation of the terrine as described above.

La poule à la béarnaise dite « au pot » de Gérard Vié

Gérard Vié, the inventor of this recipe, is the Michelin star chef of the restaurant Les Trois Marches in Versailles. He is an expert on traditional cooking and the author of *À la table des rois*.

1- Chop the Bayonne ham, the white onion, the garlic, the shallots, and the chicken livers. Combine these ingredients with the pork and the tarragon sprig, cut into 5 pieces. Fill the chicken with this stuffing. Sew the cavity closed and tie the feet together using kitchen string.

2- Immerse the chicken in a large soup pot filled with water, adding the onions stuck with the cloves. Add a large handful of sea salt and the slice of ham. Boil slowly, skimming very frequently. Peel and chop the vegetables and add them to the pot. Keep at a slow boil for 2 hours over low heat.

3- When you are ready to serve, drain the chicken. Place it on a large serving platter. Cut the chicken and the ham into 8 pieces. Mound the stuffing in the center of the platter. Arrange the vegetables and chicken and ham pieces around it. Season with salt and a generous amount of pepper. Serve very hot, accompanied by a bowl of bouillon.

Serves 4
Preparation time : 40 minutes
Cooking time : 2 hours

1 Houdan chicken, ready to cook
3 1/4 oz. Bayonne ham
1 thick slice of raw ham
4 chicken livers
5 1/4 oz. pork meat from the belly and shoulder
4 leeks, white parts only
4 carrots
4 turnips
1/2 celeriac bulb
1/2 white onion
2 large onions
2 cloves
1 garlic clove
2 shallots
1 large sprig of tarragon
coarse sea salt, regular salt, and freshly ground pepper

Le pot-au-feu

You can cook beef, duck, pork, and lamb, just as you would chicken, in a pot with vegetables.

1- Pour 3 1/4 quarts water into a soup pot. Immerse the pieces of meat in the cold water. Bring to a boil and cook 2 minutes. Drain the meat and bones in a colander and rinse them under cold water.

2- Wash out the soup pot. Pour in 3 1/4 quarts water and heat. Immerse the bones and meat in the hot water and add a handful of sea salt, 1 tablespoon of peppercorns and the *bouquet garni*. Cook 1 1/2 hours over low heat.

3- Peel the carrots, turnips, leeks, onions, and celery without cutting them up. Tie up the leeks and add all the vegetables to the pot. Let the *pot-au-feu* cook an additional 1 1/2 hours. Add the peeled potatoes 40 minutes before the end of the cooking time.

4- Cool the bouillon and skim the grease from the top. Correct the seasoning and reheat the bouillon. Arrange the meat and vegetables in a large deep platter. Accompany the *pot-au-feu* with strong Dijon mustard, cornichon pickles, and Guérande salt. Serve the bouillon piping hot alongside.

Serves 8
Preparation time : 40 minutes
Cooking time : 3 hours

1 lb., 1 oz. beef shank
8 3/4 oz. beef short ribs
14 oz. beef chuck shoulder
10 1/2 oz. top blade roast
2 lbs., 2 oz. marrow bones
5 carrots
5 turnips
2 leeks
8 large potatoes
2 onions, one stuck with two cloves
1 celery stalk
1 *bouquet garni*
1 garlic clove
coarse sea salt and peppercorns
Guérande salt and freshly ground pepper

Basquaise
in the Basque country

Onions, tomatoes, sweet pimentos, and a touch of garlic: this blend has been the foundation of Basque cuisine since the conquistadors returned from America. With this base, you can prepare whatever you wish « *à la basquaise* » : a *piperade*, a Sunday chicken, or even a tuna if you live in Saint-Jean-de-Luz.

Above
The secret of a good piperade is to quickly sauté the ingredients, without allowing them to stew or scorch.

Facing page
Returning from fishing in Saint-Jean-de-Luz. This little tuna was line-caught.

There has always been an art to cooking a *basquaise*. The onions have to be tossed in the pan over high heat, so that they neither steam nor burn. If you are cooking a chicken, this is the moment to add it to the pot, so that it gets perfectly browned and absorbs all the flavors. Only then do you add peeled tomatoes and let the whole thing simmer long and slow over low heat.

Families in Ordiarp, a village on the Soule region in the heart of Basque country, make *basquaise* daily. They might prepare it with a free-range chicken, eggs, or country ham and *ventreche*, to make a *piperade*.

Onions, tomatoes, and peppers

There has always been a *piperade* simmering in one corner of the stove, at least every other day, for as long as people in this area can remember. It is a popular summer dish, of course, when all you have to do is gather vegetables from the kitchen garden, but it is enjoyed in the winter months as well. « Putting up preserves has always been

part of the ritual of life on the farm, » explains Michel Anso, Ordiarp's mayor and innkeeper. « Containers and bottles of tomato sauce topped with a layer of oil for protection from oxidation were ubiquitous, and even eggs used to be preserved. After World War II, a new artisan set up shop in the town. When I was a child, my mother would send me to him with cans to be sealed. » It is just a small step from these recollections to making the claim that *piperade* originated in the Soule region. Michel has been considering establishing a brotherhood of knights of *piperade* in his community for some time now.

> « *You absolutely must not brutalize a* basquaise. *It has to be handled with love.* »

This idea brings a smile to faces in Basse Navarre and Labourd, the other areas that constitute the French Basque country. The trinity of vegetables—onions, tomatoes, and peppers—is the basis for all French Basque cooking. (In the area of cuisine at least, the Pyrenees do divide the Basques; in Spain they work with different seasonings.) This common theme is subject to a thousand variations: in Soule, they add breadcrumbs to the sauce for thickening, while spicy red pimentos are used in the Espelette region. Some even venture to add *cèpes* when they are in season.

Pimentos, the finest flower

La basquaise

Serves 6
Preparation : 30 minutes
Cooking time : 20 minutes

3 large onions
8 green Espelette pimentos (or 5 regular green peppers)
8 tomatoes
2 garlic cloves
1 *bouquet garni*
3 tablespoons of olive oil
1 3/4 oz. goose fat
salt and freshly milled pepper

1- Peel and chop the onions and garlic. Cut the pimentos into small pieces. Seed the tomatoes and chop them coarsely with a knife.

2- Melt the goose fat in a pot. Sauté the onions in the hot fat. Add the *bouquet garni*, the chopped garlic, the pimentos, the tomatoes and the olive oil. Season with salt and pepper and allow to cook down for 20 minutes over low heat. Serve warm.

If you replace the fresh pimentos with peppers, you may wish to add 1/2 teaspoon of dried Espelette pimento to liven up the *basquaise*.

La piperade aux œufs

You may serve this dish with thick slices of Bayonne ham sautéed in goose fat. Place the ham on top of the *piperade* just before serving.

1- Wash and chop the parsley. Beat the eggs in a large bowl. Season with salt and pepper and add the chopped parsley.
2- When you are ready to serve, melt the goose fat in a pan and pour in the beaten eggs, stirring. When the eggs begin to coagulate, add the *piperade*, and stir 5 minutes with a wooden spatula so that the eggs scramble.
3- Serve the scrambled eggs plain or on slices of country-style bread that have been rubbed with garlic and toasted.

Serves 6
Preparation time : 10 minutes
Cooking time : 10 minutes

2 lbs. cooked *basquaise*
6 eggs
1/2 bunch parsley
1 oz. goose fat
salt and pepper

Le poulet basquaise

1- Season the chicken pieces with salt and pepper, and sauté them on both sides in the melted goose fat.
2- Add the Bayonne ham slivers and 1 cup of water, then the *piperade*. Simmer 45 minutes, stirring frequently. Serve hot.

Variation
You may also prepare tuna *basquaise* using this method. Select 6 tuna filets, each weighing about 6 oz. Allow only 15 minutes cooking time.

Serves 6
Preparation time : 40 minutes
Cooking time : 45 minutes

6 chicken legs
7 oz. slivered Bayonne ham
3 1/2 oz. goose fat
2 lbs. cooked basquaise
salt and pepper

took on a distinctive character, with an elongated shape and a mellow, complex flavor carefully bred by the Basques. It would be heretical to substitute standard peppers for these pimentos, which have established their place in the vast vegetable family of more than 2000 species. Connoisseurs call it the « Anglet pimento », because before the expanding cities of Bayonne, Anglet, and Biarritz nibbled away at farmlands, most fishermen lived in Anglet. Here, this is the standard, garden variety pimento. The Espelette pimento, now protected by an AOC, is used very sparingly, rather like black pepper.

> « Basques have always been sailors or adventurers, whichever side of the border they're from. »

A tribute to tuna and the Luz region

The return of the pimento to the seaside is an historical curiosity. Old fishermen tend to remember eating tuna prepared « en marmitako », a sort of stew, or simply fried and served with slow cooked onions; these days, however, tuna *basquaise* figures prominently on every menu in Saint-Jean-de-Luz. You can do even better at the Tuna Festival in July, when all of the city's sports leagues offer an array of tuna dishes to taste for one price. There are numerous clubs–judo, rugby, and basketball. The vital energy of the Basque countryside unites around tuna *basquaise*, a dish unheard of 30 years ago.

This picture represents the soul of the Basque country. In the not-so-distant post-war period, tuna fishing was the glory of Saint-Jean-de-Luz. Every summer, ten to fifteen men would pile into little boats to fish for tuna with rods behind the sea wall. The harvest was miraculous. Back in the harbor, the boats would line up in a chain to unload the gleaming silver fish. Vendors paid for them with cash and throngs of tourists flocked around. Blue boats filled the boat basins, and there were canneries everywhere on the quays. The streets of Ciboure across the bay smelled of fish, and the bells of factories seeking laborers would wake you at dawn. The city revolved around tuna. The Basque country had found itself a treasure. What better tribute than to dress it up as they always had chicken and ham, *à la basquaise*.

Above

Near Arbonne. Charles Borda, a grower, cultivates sweet « Anglat » pimentos. These pimentos (which are not peppers) are an essential ingredient in any self-respecting piperade.

Facing page

The tuna festival at Saint-Jean-de-Luz. Every civic organization in town has its own stand serving grilled tuna accompanied by a sauce basquaise. This is a tradition that goes back over thirty years.

of the pepper family

The paradox of this nationally popular dish, which seems so firmly rooted in the Basque country, is that it is really a recent immigrant from across the sea. Garlic and onion are certainly among the oldest vegetables cultivated in France. Tomatoes, however, came to us from Mexico in the sixteenth century, and the pepper sailed back with Christopher Columbus. Is there a Spanish influence? André Darraidou is so ardent a proponent of Espelette pimentos that he has covered the entire façade of his hotel with them. He shrugs the question aside. « History does not tell us if the first importers of pimentos had the surname of Roblès or Etcheverry.»

Moving inland from ocean ports, the pepper found its way into kitchen gardens. In the interior, people combined the roles of farmer and fisherman, just as in Brittany. Over the course of centuries, pimentos

Le thon basquaise nouvelle cuisine de Grégoire Sein

In Basque country markets, you can ask your fishmonger for an exceptionally succulent and unusual pear-shaped filet of tuna that is cut from the head above the gills. These filets are perfectly suited for the cooking method and seasonings of this recipe.

Serves 4
Preparation time : 35 minutes
Cooking time : 40 minutes

1 lb., 5 oz. tuna filet
6 thin slices of Bayonne ham
3 large onions
6 green onions
3 garlic cloves
2 bay leaves
2 Espelette pimentos
a few sprigs of Italian parsley
6 tablespoons olive oil
1 tablespoon cider vinegar
salt and pepper

1- Finely chop the pimentos, the large onions, and the green onions, setting aside their sprouts. Peel the garlic and wash and mince the parsley. Wash the green onion sprouts and keep them whole.

2- Cut the tuna into 6 thick pieces. Wrap each piece in a slice of Bayonne ham and then wrap each packet in aluminum foil.

3- Heat 3 tablespoons of the olive oil in a pot. Sauté the onions for 2 minutes. Season with salt and pepper. Add the bay leaves and brown the onions for 10 minutes over low heat. Add the green onion sprouts and the pimentos and cook 10 minutes more. Preheat the oven to 320°.

4- Heat a non-stick pan. In it sauté the pieces of fish and ham, wrapped in the aluminum foil, without adding any fat. Cook them on all sides, then bake the packets for 5 minutes.

5- Remove the aluminum foil. Add the tuna pieces to the pot with the onion mixture and let the ingredients simmer over low heat for 5 minutes. The tuna should still be rare in the middle. Arrange the pieces of tuna and the onion-pimento mixture on a large platter and keep warm.

6- When you are ready to serve, heat the rest of the olive oil in the same pot you used to cook the onions. Sauté the garlic in the hot oil. Deglaze the pan with the vinegar, cook 30 seconds, and add the parsley. Drizzle these juices over the tuna and onions. Serve immediately with a red wine from Irouleguy.

Le thon rouge mariné aux piments d'Espelette

A *basquaise* is delicious served cold, and tuna is often eaten uncooked. This recipe makes the most of both ingredients.

1- Cut the tuna into 24 fairly thin slices. (You can simplify this step by slightly freezing the tuna in advance, as you would for a *carpaccio*.) Place the slices in the refrigerator. Cut the red pepper and the pimentos into small dice. Peel and chop the onions and garlic. Wash and roughly chop the basil.
2- Heat 1 3/4 oz. of the olive oil in a sauté pan. Sauté the onions, garlic, peppers, and pimento. Season with salt and pepper and allow the mixture to cook down over low heat, stirring frequently, for 20 minutes. When this *ratatouille* is cooked, add the chopped basil. Correct the seasoning and cool in a large bowl.
3- In another bowl, whisk together the lemon juice, the vinegar and the rest of the olive oil. Season with salt and pepper.
4- 10 minutes before serving, arrange the tuna slices on a large earthenware dish. Sprinkle them with the marinade and let them « cook »5 minutes.
5- When you are ready to serve, arrange a slice of the marinated tuna on each plate. Cover with a spoonful of the *ratatouille*, and place another slice of tuna on top. Repeat this step two more times. Serve as a first course with a small hearts of lettuce salad seasoned with fresh herbs.

Serves 6
Preparation time : 40 minutes
Cooking time : 20 minutes

1 lb., 1 oz. red tuna filet
3 Espelette pimentos
2 onions
1 red pepper
3 garlic cloves
1 bunch of basil
juice of 1 lemon
3 1/2 oz. olive oil
1 oz. sherry vinegar
salt and pepper

Pays d'Oc

L'ouillade

Serves 6
Preparation time : 30 minutes
Soaking time : 2 hours
Cooking time : 2 hours

1 pork hock
1/2 green cabbage
10 1/2 oz. white beans
3 potatoes
2 carrots
1 leek
1 *bouquet garni*
1 3/4 oz. butter
1 3/4 oz. olive oil
6 slices country-style bread toasted
salt and pepper

1- Soak the white beans for 2 hours in cold water. Cook them without seasoning for 1 hour over low heat in their soaking water. Meanwhile, immerse the pork hock in 1 1/2 quarts cold water and simmer 1 hour over low heat.
2- Peel the carrots and onions and cut them into thick rounds. Wash and mince the leek. Combine the pork, beans, carrots, cabbage, leek, and potatoes in a soup pot and pour over the cooking liquid from the pork. Add the *bouquet garni*. Season with salt and pepper and simmer 1 additional hour over low heat.

3- Turn off the heat. Stir the butter and olive oil into the soup. Correct the seasonings. This dish is presented as two courses. First serve the bouillon over slices of toasted bread, followed by the meat and vegetables in the same plate. Enjoy very hot!

Bassin d'Arcachon

Les huîtres aux crépinettes

Serves 6
Preparation time : 50 minutes
Soaking time : 30 minutes
Cooking time : 20 minutes

24 oysters from the Arcachon basin
14 oz. sausage meat
3 oz. caul
3 oz. butter
1 oz. truffles
8 1/2 oz. white wine

1- Place the caul in cold water to soak for 30 minutes. Drain it and dry it in a cloth. Cut it into 12 squares about 4-inches on each side.
2- Chop the truffle and mix with the sausage meat. Place small mounds of the sausage mixture on the pieces of caul. Fold in the edges and seal them carefully.
3- Melt the butter in a pan. Sauté the *crépinettes* in the hot butter. Turn

them over and cook for 10 minutes without browning. Pour over the white wine and simmer 5 minutes more.
4- Drain the *crépinettes* and keep them warm. Open the oysters and eat them one by one, alternating with a *crépinette* and a swallow of white Graves.

Périgord

Le foie gras d'oie à la périgourdine

Serves 6
Preparation time : 20 minutes
Soaking time : 12 hours
Refrigeration time : 20 minutes
Cooking time : 1 hour

1 goose *foie gras*, weighing about 12 oz.
3 1/2 oz. truffles
1 piece of barding fat (or a thin slice of smoked pork belly)
2 1/2 oz. goose fat
1 onion
2 shallots
1 tablespoon flour
1 oz. white wine
1 oz. chicken bouillon (You may use bouillon cubes.)
salt and pepper

1- The day before you prepare the dish, put the *foie gras* in cold water and soak it overnight. Drain it and dry with a cloth. Season with salt and pepper.

2- Cut the truffles into small slivers and carefully insert them into the *foie gras*. Let it rest for 20 minutes in the refrigerator, covered with a cloth. Preheat the oven to 250°.
3- Cover the *foie gras* with the barding fat, brush with 1 3/4 oz. of the goose fat and wrap it in a sheet of greaseproof paper. Tie this package together with string and bake it in the oven for 40 minutes, basting it regularly with cooking fat.
4- Meanwhile, peel and mince the onions and shallots. Melt the rest of the goose fat and sauté the onion and shallots in the hot fat. Cook 5 minutes over low heat, and stir in the flour. Pour in the white wine and the chicken bouillon. Season with salt and pepper. Simmer 10 minutes over low heat.
5- Remove the *foie gras* from the oven and place it on a serving platter. Correct the seasoning of the sauce. Pour the sauce around the *foie gras* and serve very hot.

Le gâteau aux noix

Serves 6
Preparation time : 20 minutes
Cooking time : 40 minutes

4 oz. walnut meats, plus 1 1/2 oz. for decorating
4 oz. ground almonds
4 1/2 oz. butter, softened and cut into small pieces
10 1/2 oz. granulated sugar
5 eggs
3 oz. flour
2 tablespoons of rum
1/3 oz. unsweetened cocoa powder
1 3/4 oz. confectioners' sugar

1- Preheat the oven to 410°. Chop 4 oz. of the walnut meats in a food processor. In a large bowl, whisk together the butter and eggs, adding them one by one. Whisk in the sugar.
2- Add the chopped walnuts and ground almonds, then whisk again to blend thoroughly. Fold in the rum and flour with a spatula.
3- Butter springform pan and pour in the batter. Bake the cake for 40 minutes. When it is browned and firm to the touch, take it out of the oven and let it cool before removing it from the baking pan. Place the cake on a serving plate and decorate it with the remaining walnut halves. Sprinkle confectioners sugar and cocoa on top before serving.

Aquitaine

Les entrecôtes sauce bordelaise

Serves 6
Preparation time : 30 minutes
Cooking time : 1 hour

6 rib steaks
10 shallots
3 oz. red Bordeaux wine
1 sprig of thyme
5 oz. butter
a few sprigs of parsley
salt and pepper

1- Light your barbecue grill and let the coals burn for 45 minutes to reach a good heat. Peel and chop the shallots. Wash and chop the parsley. Melt 3 oz. of the butter in a large pot and add the shallots and the thyme sprig. Cook 10 minutes over low heat without allowing the mixture to brown. Pour over the red wine and reduce the sauce to 1/4 of its original volume. Remove from the heat. Whisk in the remaining butter. Season with salt and pepper.
2- Grill the steaks 5 minutes on each side. Season with salt and pepper, sprinkle with the parsley and arrange on a serving platter. Cover the steaks with the *sauce bordelaise* and serve.

Catalogne

La morue à la catalane

Serves 6
Preparation time : 20 minutes
Soaking time : 24 hours
Cooking time : 1 hour

2 lbs., 2 oz. salt cod (You may also use lightly salted fresh cod filets; in this case, allow only 2 hours soaking time.)
5 anchovies preserved in salt
3 1/2 oz. olive oil
1 lb., 1 ounce potatoes
4 tomatoes
3 garlic cloves
1 onion
1 *bouquet garni*
8 1/2 oz. dry white wine
pepper

1- Soak the salt cod and the anchovies in cold water for 24 hours, changing the water as often as possible.
2- The day you plan to serve the dish, peel and chop the onions. Crush the garlic cloves in their skins. Cut the tomatoes into large cubes. Peel the potatoes and cut them into rounds.
3- Heat the olive oil in a pot. Add the onion, garlic, *bouquet garni*, and the anchovies. Arrange the potato rounds and tomatoes over the top. Add the white wine and 8 1/2 oz. water and cook 35 minutes over very low heat, stirring occasionally.
4- When the potatoes are cooked, season the mixture with pepper. Cut the cod into 6 pieces. Add the cod to the pot and cook, covered, another 20 minutes. Serve the cod, garnished with the vegetables, and moistened with the cooking juices.

Pays Basque

Les chipirons à l'encre

Serves 6
Preparation time : 30 minutes
Cooking time : 1 hour 45 minutes

5 lbs., 5 oz. squid, cleaned and ready to cook
1 3/4 oz. squid ink (sold in specialty grocery shops or by your fishmonger)
3 onions
8 garlic cloves
4 tomatoes
1 *bouquet garni*
a few sprigs of parsley
1/2 teaspoon ground Espelette pimento
1 3/4 oz. olive oil
17 oz. white wine
salt and pepper

1- Cut each squid into 4 pieces. Peel and chop the onion and garlic cloves. Heat the olive oil in a pot. Sauté the onions in the oil, stirring.
2- When the onions are browned, add the squid, the garlic, the pimento, and the *bouquet garni*. Season with salt and pepper and cook 5 minutes more. Add the tomatoes, cut into large cubes, the ink, and the white wine. Simmer gently for 1 1/2 hours.
3- When the squid are well cooked and tender, turn off the heat. Correct the seasoning and add the chopped parsley. Serve very hot.

Le gâteau basque

Serves 4
Preparation time : 30 minutes
Resting time : 15 minutes
Cooking time : 40 minutes

3 eggs
3 1/2 oz. granulated sugar, plus 3/4 oz. vanilla flavored sugar
4 1/4 oz. butter, softened
3 1/2 oz. flour
1 ounce ground almonds
1/10 oz. baking powder
1 tablespoon rum
4 drops bitter almond extract
10 1/2 oz. *crème pâtissière* or 7 oz. black cherry preserves
salt

1- Sift the flour into a large bowl. Make a well in the center and add the baking powder, a pinch of salt, the ground almonds, the rum, and the bitter almond flavoring. Combine thoroughly.
2- In another bowl, beat 2 of the eggs vigorously, then add the granulated sugar and the vanilla flavored sugar. Fold in 3 1/2 oz. of the butter in small pieces, then add the contents of the first bowl. Let the batter rest for 15 minutes. Preheat the oven to 320°.
3- Butter a springform pan about 8-inches in diameter. Cover the bottom with half the batter, evening it out the top with the back of a spoon. Pour over a thick layer of *crème pâtissière* or preserves to within 1/2 inch of the edge.
4- Pour over the rest of the batter and even out the surface. Beat the remaining egg and brush over the top to make a glaze. Bake the cake for 40 minutes.

Travel notes

Here are the addresses of the people who shared their cooking secrets with us and allowed us to sample their specialties.

Olivier Roellinger
(recipe on page 15)
Les Maisons de Bricourt
Rue Du Guesclin
35260 Cancale
Tel: 02 99 89 64 76

Christian Constant
(recipe on page 20)
Restaurant Le Violon
d'Ingres
135, rue Saint-Dominique
75007 Paris
Tel: 01 45 55 15 05

Jacques Thorel
(recipe on page 34)
L'Auberge bretonne
2, place Du Guesclin
56130 La Roche-Bernard

Alain Passard
(recipe on page 50)
L'Arpège
84, rue de Varenne
75007 Paris
Tel: 01 47 05 09 06

Émile Jung
(recipe on page 68)
Le Crocodile
10, rue Outre
37000 Strasbourg
Tel: 03 88 32 13 02

Michel Bras
(recipe on page 96)
Restaurant Michel Bras
Le Puech de Suquet
12210 Laguiole
Tel: 05 65 51 18 20

François Rongier
(recipe on page 96)
Chalet du Col de Serre
15400 Le Claux
Tel: 04 71 78 93 97

Gaby
(recipe on page 112)
Grand Bar des Goudes
Rue Désiré-Pellaprat
13008 Marseille
Tel: 04 91 73 43 69

Joël Passédat
(recipe on page 117)
Le Petit Nice
Anse de Maldormé
13007 Marseille
Tel: 04 91 59 25 92

Madame Hugon
(recipe on page 129)
Chez Hugon
12, rue Pizay
69001 Lyon

Dominique Le Stanc
(recipe on page 137)
La Mérenda
4, rue de la Terrasse
06300 Nice
No telephone number
because reservations are not
accepted.

Alain Llorca
(recipe on page 140)
Restaurant le Chantecler
Hôtel le Négresco
37, promenade des Anglais
06000 Nice

Antoine Casanova
(recipe on page 144)
Pâtisserie Casanova
6, cours Paoli
20250 Corte
Tel: 04 95 46 00 79

Dominique Toulousy
(recipe on page 160)
Les Jardins de l'Opéra
1, place du Capitole
31000 Toulouse
Tel: 05 61 23 07 76

Hélène Darroze
(recipe on page 168)
Restaurant Hélène Darroze
4, rue d'Assas
75006 Paris
Tel: 01 42 22 00 11

Bernard Coudouy
(recipe on page 172)
L'Arrégalet
37, rue du Bourguet
64440 Laruns
Tel: 05 59 05 35 47

Gérard Vié
(recipe on page 177)
Les Trois Marches
Hôtel Trianon Palace
1, boulevard de la Reine
78000 Versailles

The addresses below are not intended to be a comprehensive touring guide. They are our travel notes and include some of the pleasant surprises we encountered in the course of our research.

Le homard à l'armoricaine

L'ETRAVE
29770 Cléden-Cap-Sizun
Tel: 02 98 70 66 87
People come here primarily to savor the *ragoût de homard* in a sauce enriched with coral. Servings are generous.

La sole normande

LES ARCADES
1, arcade de la Bourse
76200 Dieppe
Tel: 02 35 84 14 12
This homestyle restaurant in Dieppe features an excellent *sole dieppoise tradition* on its menu.

À LA MARMITE DIEPPOISE
8, rue Saint-Jean
76200 Dieppe
Tel: 02 35 84 24 26
Regrettably, *sole normande* appears only occasionally on the menus of formal restaurants in Dieppe. However, this restaurant offers a *marmite dieppoise* (with a variety of different fish), a dish that the staff will assure you was invented here.

Les crêpes bretonnes

CRÊPERIE TY-GWECHALL
4, rue Mellac
29300 Quimperlé
Tel: 02 98 96 30 63
The chef in this restaurant uses *crêpes* as a base for a wide variety of delicious accompaniments: filet of whiting with sorrel puree, warm Merrien oysters, chutney, and seaweed.

LA TAUPINIÈRE
Croissant Saint-André
29930 Pont-Aven
Tel: 02 98 06 03 12
Crêpes are among the ingredients used here in a true connoisseur's kitchen.

BISCUITERIE DE QUIMPER STIVELL
8, rue du Chanoine-Moreau
29000 Quimper
Tel: 02 98 53 10 13
Located in the historic district of Quimper, this cookie factory carries on the traditional baking of *crêpes dentelles*. You can observe the production process and sample the results.

La tarte aux pommes

LA BOURRIDE
15, rue Vaugueux
14000 Caen
Tel: 02 31 93 50 76
The chef here is among the few who give equal time to desserts. He loves apples and prepares them in every way imaginable.

Les moules-frites

BRASSERIE AUX MOULES
34, rue de Béthune
59800 Lille
Tel: 03 20 57 12 45
This classic haunt for *moules-frites* becomes a major attraction during the summer outdoor festival known as the « braderie ».

HET BLAUWERZHOF
9, rue Eecke
59270 Godewaersvelde
Tel: 03 28 49 45 11
More *coqs à la biere* than *moules-frites* are served in this tavern in the Flemish hills. However, the *frites* are an excellent daily special here.

La gratinée à l'oignon

LA POULE AU POT
9, rue Vauvilliers
75001 Paris
Tel: 01 42 36 32 96
This is an old Parisian bistro where you can fortify yourself all night long with an onion soup or a *poule au pot*.

AU PIED DE COCHON
6, rue Coquellière
75001 Paris
Tel: 01 40 13 77 00
Once located across from the meat pavilion of the old Les Halles, this restaurant, open 24 hours a day 7 days a week, still attracts a throng of nocturnal diners.

La choucroute

RESTAURANT CHEZ PHILIPPE
8, place de l'Église
67113 Blaesheim
Tel: 03 88 68 86 00
Every conceivable variation on *choucroute* is available here—including one based on Vietnamese noodles.

MAISON KAMMERZELL
16, place de la Cathédrale
67000 Strasbourg
Tel: 03 88 32 42 14
In this old building across from the cathedral, Guy-Pierre Bommard has restored the popularity of *choucroute* prepared with fish.

Le boeuf bourguignon

HÔTEL-RESTAURANT DE LA POSTE
71600 Poisson
Tel: 03 85 81 10 72
In southern Burgundy between the Brionnais and Charolais regions, Jean-Noël Dauvergne, a native son, prepares delicacies featuring Charolais beef in many themes and variations.

L'estofinado

LA BEAUSÉJOUR
Le bourg
15340 Calvinet
Tel: 04 71 49 91 68
Estofinado, updated and enhanced by a talented chef, is offered in season, along with oxtails from Salers and stuffed cabbage with a reduction of wine from Marcillac.

RESTAURANT DRUILHES
40, avenue Paul-Ramadier
12300 Livinhac-le-Haut
Tel: 05 65 63 35 65
Two little ladies prepare traditional *estofinado* in their inn on the banks of the Lot.

RESTAURANT CARRIER
12300 Almon-les-Junies
Tel: 05 65 44 10 41
One of the establishments
that contributes to Almon-
les-Junies' vaunted reputation as the « world capital of
estofinado. »

**The cooking of the
Auvergne:** *aligot, truffade*
and *potée*

HOTEL DE LA DOMERIE
12470 Aubrac
Tel: 05 65 44 28 42
A good spot to sample a generous *aligot.* You could also
try the place across the street
(Hôtel Aubrac) where the
legendary Germaine
presided for many years.

BEL HORIZON
15800 Vic-sur-Cère
Tel: 04 71 47 50 06
Here you will find *truffades*
and *aligot*s, as well as kid
with chanterelle mushrooms
and perch with Planèze
lentils.

L'AUBRAC
17, allée de l'Amicale
12210 Laguiole
Tel: 05 65 44 32 13
Every Sunday here, there is a
celebration with a giant
aligot, stirred with a real
workman's shovel.

La bouillabaisse

LE MIRAMAR
12, quai du Port
13002 Marseille
Tel: 04 91 91 10 40
The classic *bouillabaisse* of
Marseille in the heart of the
Vieux Port district.

CHEZ FONFON
140, vallon des Auffes
13007 Marseille
Tel: 04 91 52 14 38
The legendary address for
the *bouillabaisse* in Marseille.
Fonfon's nephew has perpet-
uated the tradition since his
uncle's death.

La fondue

**AUBERGE
DE LA CÔTE 2000**
Route de la Côte 2000
74120 Megève
Tel: 04 50 21 31 84
One of the good restaurants
in this resort.

Le poulet de Bresse

GEORGES BLANC
Place du marché
01540 Vonnas
Tel: 04 74 50 90 90
The true aristocrat of *poulet
de Bresse.*

**RESTAURANT LA MAISON
DU POULET DE BRESSE**
Route départementale 875
71470 Romenay
Tel: 03 85 40 33 48
In the capital of *poulet de
Bresse* (in Burgundian
Bresse), this is an excellent
and reasonably priced
restaurant.

La pissaladière

CHEZ THERESA
Every morning, you will find
the queen of Niçoise
pissaldière and *socca* in the
market on Cours Saleya in
Nice.

Le fiadone

U SCOGLIU
Marine de Cannelle
20217 Canari
Tel: 04 95 37 80 06
The setting, at the end of a
small inlet on Cap Corse, is
breathtaking. The menu is
worthy of the view, and the
fiadone is its climax.

Le cassoulet

HOSTELLERIE ETIENNE
1, chemin Saint-Jammes
11320 Labastide-d'Anjou
Tel: 04 68 60 10 08
One of the best *cassoulet*s in
the Castelnaudary style,
slowly baked for seven hours
by one of the distinguished
men of the region, Etienne
Rousselot.

Le confit

JACKY CARLES
La Table paysanne
12200 Monteils
Tel: 05 65 29 62 39
Sample traditional country
dishes and purchase *confits*
prepared in a copper
cauldron.

M. ET MME. BÉGUÉ
Laoueillée
32120 Bajonnette
Tel: 05 62 06 84 39
Traditionally prepared *foie
gras* and *confits.*

LE BISTROT D'EN-FACE
24510 Tremolat
Tel: 05 53 22 80 69
An excellent source for
confits.

La poule au pot

**FERME-AUBERGE MARYSE
ET ELIZABETH BISCAR**
Rue d'Église
64230 Arbus
Tel: 05 59 83 12 31
15 kilometers from Pau,
there is a weekly gathering of
poule au pot devotees at this
lovely farm in the Béarnaise
countryside. Reserve ahead.

*La basquaise and its
variations*

RESTAURANT OSTALAPIA
2621 chemin Ostalapea
64210 Ahetze
Tel: 05 59 54 73 79
Tuna, *piperade,* and other
Basque specialties can be
sampled in the mountainside
garden here during the summer months.

**HÔTEL-RESTAURANT
LE GARAÏBIE**
Françoise et Jean Anso
64130 Ordiarp
Tel: 05 59 28 18 85
6 kilometers from Ordiarp
and seemingly at the end
of the world, this restaurant
serves excellent family
cooking.

EUZKADI
64250 Espelette
Tel: 05 59 93 91 88
A village inn owned by an
avid booster of Espelette
pimentos, who doubles as
the town's mayor. People
come here for the *piperade,*
l'axoa (chopped lamb shoulder), and the *gâteau basque.*

Index of recipes with English translations

Aïoli (garlic mayonnaise) 151

Aligot (pureed potatoes with cheese) 93

Artichaut à la bretonne (artichokes braised in cider) 44

Baekenofe (casserole of potatoes and four varieties of meat) 71

Basquaise (tomato, onion, and pepper stew) 180

Boeuf bourguignon (beef stew with red wine) 76

Boeuf en daube (beef braised with Provençal red wine) 150

Bouillabaisse d'oeufs (eggs poached in a tomato vegetable sauce) 116

Bouillabaisse de poissons à la marseillaise (classic fish bouillabaisse) 112

Bouillabaisse de volaille et langouste (bouillabaisse with chicken and crayfish) 117

Bourguignon de légumes aux herbes potagères (vegetables cooked with red wine) 80

Brandade de morue pommes vapeur (salt cod puree with potatoes) 89

Brochet au bleu (poached pike) 107

Bugnes (fritters flavored with rum and lemon) 106

Calissons d'Aix (almond confections from Aix) 150

Casse-museau (whole apples baked in pastry) 42

Cassoulet (slow baked bean and meat casserole) 156

Cassoulet aux fèves de Dominique Toulousy (*cassoulet* with fava beans) 160

Cassoulet de morue (*cassoulet* with salt cod) 161

Cassoulet léger de homard à l'estragon (*cassoulet* with lobster and tarragon) 160

Cervelle de canut (herbed cheese spread) 106

Chipirons à l'encre (calamari stewed in their own ink) 187

Chou farci (stuffed cabbage) 104

Choucroute (sauerkraut and meat casserole) 64

Choucroute de chou rouge et pigeon à la chinoise (red cabbage *choucroute* with pigeon, seasoned with Chinese spices) 69

Choucroute de poisson (*choucroute* with fish) 68

Clémentines soufflées au fiadone (clementines with a soufflé filling) 148

Compressé de bouillabaisse (chilled fish and *bouillabaisse* mold) 117

Confit de canard (duck conserve) 164

Confit de poire au miel (pears poached in honey syrup) 168

Coq à la bière (rooster stewed in beer) 70

Coq au vin (rooster stewed in red wine) 80

Côtes de veau à la normande (veal chops with mushrooms in cream sauce) 45

Crêpes (traditional thin pancakes) 28

Crêpes dentelles de Jacques Thorel (lacy rolled baked crêpes) 34

Crêpes légères à la cannelle et au miel caramélisé (crêpes with cinnamon-flavored caramelized honey sauce) 35

Crostinis à la fondue d'oignons rouges caramélisés (warm canapés with caramelized onions and parmesan) 58

Cuisses de grenouilles poêlées et mille choux à la coriandre d'Emile Jung (frogs' legs with cabbage, sauerkraut, and coriander) 68

Entrecôtes sauce bordelaise (rib steaks with red wine sauce) 187

Estoficado (dried cod and vegetables cooked with tomatoes) 88

Estofinado (dried cod and potato casserole) 84

Far au pruneaux (prune and raisin cake) 44

Fiadone (flourless cheese and lemon cake from Corsica) 144

Filets de sole à la dieppoise (sole with mushrooms and shellfish in cream sauce) 24

Flammenküche (onion and bacon tart) 71

Foie gras d'oie à la périgourdine (baked truffled *foie gras* with onion and shallot sauce) 186

Foie gras des Landes confit aux épices douces d'Hélène Darroze (*foie gras* conserve with sweet spices and fruit chutney) 168

Fondue de poireaux sauce dieppoise (shellfish with creamy leek sauce) 24

Fondue savoyarde (traditional cheese fondue) 122

Fritures de moules et la purée de pommes de terre à la fourchette (fried breaded mussels with potato puree) 54

Galette d'aligot à la viande d'Aubrac marinée à la gentiane (pancakes made with pureed potatoes with cheese and marinated beef) 93

Galettes (buckwheat pancakes) 28

Gâteau aux noix (walnut cake) 186

Gâteau basque (almond butter cake) 187

Gougères (warm gruyère puffs) 106

Gratinée à l'oignon (onion soup topped with melted cheese) 58

Homard à l'armoricane (lobster with tomato cream sauce) 14

Huîtres aux crépinettes (sausage canapés to accompany raw oysters) 186

Kig-ha farz (beef and vegetable stew with buckwheat and prune boiled pudding) 44

Kouglof (sweet yeast cake with raisins and almonds) 71

Kouing amann (Breton sour dough cake) 44

Maquereaux au vin blanc ou au cidre (mackerel baked in cider or white wine) 45

Migliacci « Casanova » (yeast cakes prepared with lemon and cheese) 144

Morue à la catalane (salt cod stewed with potatoes in tomato sauce) 187

Moules marinières et pommes de terre frites (mussels cooked in white wine, served with French fried potatoes) 50

Moules marinières infusées à la verveine d'Alain Passard (mussels cooked in an infusion of verbena) 50

Omelette de la mère Poulard (traditional omelet from Mont-Saint-Michel) 45

Ouillade (hearty bean and cabbage soup with ham) 186

Pannequets au fromage (crêpes filled with béchamel sauce and cheese) 34

Pâté limousin (sausage and potato pâté in a crust) 107

Patranque du Col de Serre (seasoned toast with creamy cheese sauce) 96

Petits farcis (stuffed onions, tomatoes, and zucchini) 151

Petits homards d'Olivier Roellinger (small lobsters cooked with spices) 15

Pieds de porc Sainte-Menehould (breaded baked pigs' feet) 71

Piperade aux oeufs (eggs scrambled with *piperade*) 181

Pissaladière (onion, olive, and anchovy tart) 137

Pissaladière de rougets d'Alain Llorca (chickpea flour fritters with poached fish) 140

Pissalat (anchovy condiment) 137

Polenta de châtaigne (chestnut flour polenta) 150

Pot-au-feu (beef cooked with vegetables in bouillon) 177

Potée auvergnate (sausages, pork, and cabbage cooked in bouillon) 101

Potée de chou et haddock (haddock and cabbage cooked in bouillon) 104

Poulard à la crème (chicken in cream sauce) 129

Poularde de Bresse aux échalottes confites en cocotte lutée (chicken slow baked in a sealed casserole) 129

Poularde demi-deuil de la mère Brasier (poached chicken flavored with truffles) 132

Poularde pochée à la crème ou « sauce suprême » (poached chicken in cream sauce) 132

Poule à la béarnaise dite « au pot » de Gérard Vié (stuffed poached chicken with vegetables) 177

Poule au pot (stuffed poached chicken with rice pilaf and two sauces) 172

Poulet basquaise (chicken stewed with tomatoes, onions, and peppers) 181

Poulet vallée d'Auge (chicken with Calvados cream sauce) 45

Quiche lorraine (egg and bacon tart) 70

Salade de fruits de mer, vinaigrette à l'armoricaine (salad of shrimp and scallops in seasoned vinaigrette) 15

Salade de pommes de terre et saucisson chaud à la pistache façon « coco » (warm potato and pistachio sausage salad) 106

Sardines farcies au brocciu (sardines stuffed with Corsican cheese) 150

Sole normande (sole with shellfish and mushrooms in cream sauce) 20

Soufflé de morue aux pommes de terre à l'huile de noix (salt cod and potato soufflé with walnut oil) 89

Soupe au chou (cabbage soup) 101

Soupe crémeuse de fromage et pomme de terre au pain brûlé (creamy cheese and potato soup with seasoned breadcrumbs) 122

Soupe de blé noir (buckwheat flour soup) 44

Tarte à l'oignon gratinée (onion, ham, and cheese tart) 59

Tarte au sucre (sugar tart) 70

Tarte aux pommes à la normande (flambéed apple tart) 39

Tarte qui cuit deux fois (twice-baked apple custard tart) 39

Tartelettes fines aux pommes râpées (crunchy apple tartlets) 42

Tartiflette (melted cheese on a base of crisp potatoes and ham) 123

Terrine du pot infusée à l'estragon (chilled chicken and vegetable mold seasoned with tarragon) 176

Thon basquaise nouvelle cuisine de Grégoire Sein (tuna filets and Bayonne ham with pimentos and onion) 184

Thon rouge mariné aux piments d'Espelette (marinated sliced raw tuna with pimentos, peppers, and onions) 185

Tian provençal (baked tomatoes and zucchini topped with cheese) 151

Tomates froides farcies de pissalat et fondue d'oignons (tomatoes stuffed with anchovy condiment and slow-cooked onions) 140

Tripoux de Laguiole (slowly poached stuffed veal scallops) 107

Truffade (sautéed potatoes with melted cheese and cream) 93

Voyage de l'aligot de Michel Bras (cheese pancakes with potato puree and walnuts) 96

Waterzooï de poulet (poached chicken and vegetables with cream sauce) 70